THE GIFT OF TAI CHI

MICHAEL KASPER

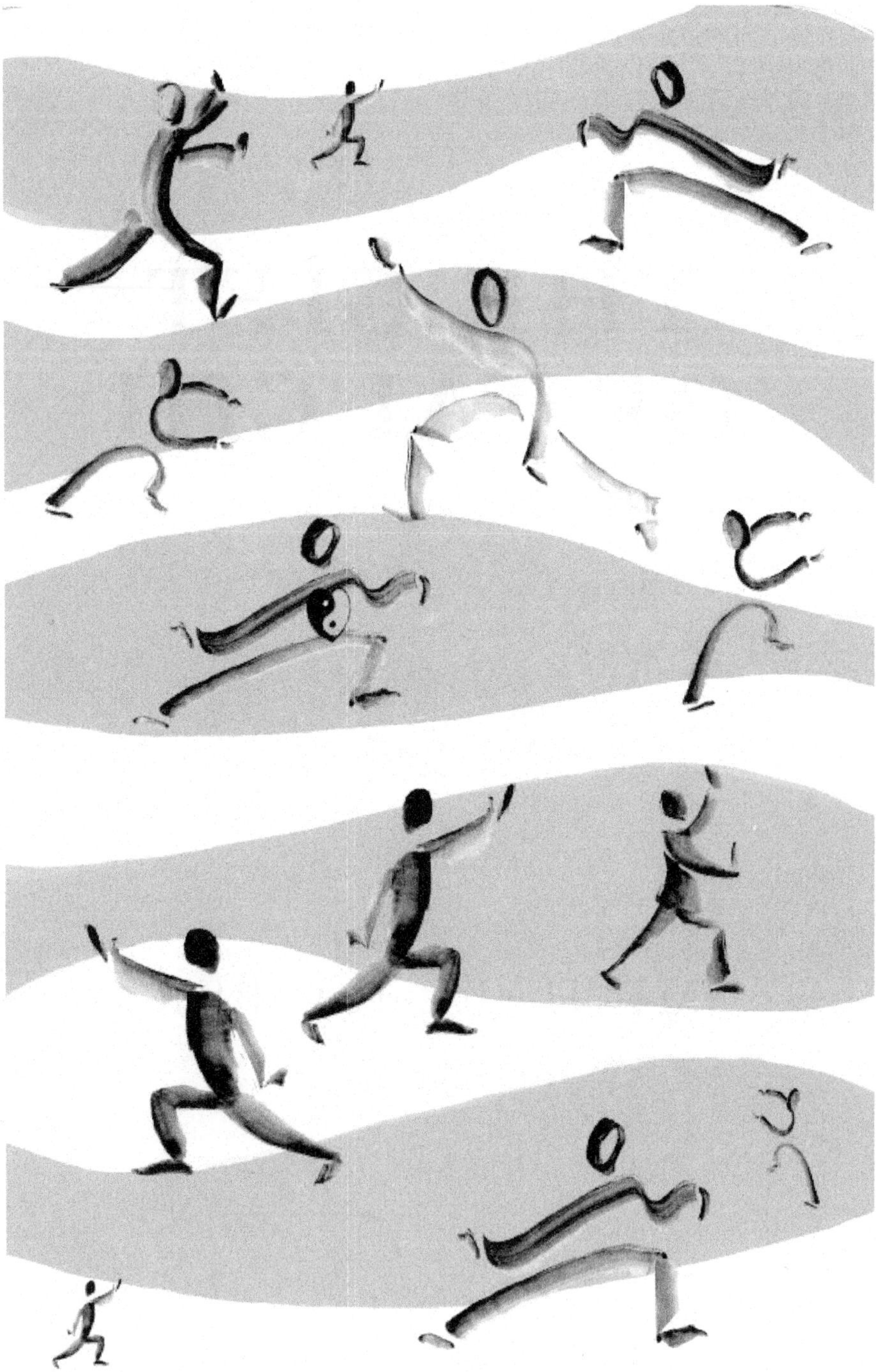

For Erika,
All best regards,
[signature] 7/15/17

Copyright © 2016 by Michael Kasper.

All rights reserved. No part of this book may be reproduced in any written, electronic, recording, or photocopying without written permission of the publisher or author. The exception would be in the case of brief quotations embodied in articles or reviews and pages where permission is specifically granted by the publisher or author.

Michael Kasper/The Gift of Tai Chi
Printed in the United States of America

Illustrations and artwork: Maria Valladarez

Although every precaution has been taken to verify the accuracy of the information contained herein, the author and publisher assume no responsibility for any errors or omissions. No liability is assumed for damages that may result from the use of information contained within.

The Gift of Tai Chi/ Michael Kasper. -- 1st ed.

ISBN 978-0-9963966-5-3 Print Edition

CONTENTS

Note from the Author vii
Introduction xi
The Gift 1
Shadow Tai Chi 5
Tai Chi Comes to a Child 9
Tai Chi and the Sea 13
Empty Space 17
The Surprised Thief in Barcelona 21
Finding the Music Underneath 25
Talking to the Animals 29
Beautiful Hawaii 33
As Above . . . So Below 37
Qigong vs. Tai Chi 41
When Is It Mine? 45
The Vortex and Our Spiraling Energy 49
The Golfer 57
Raising Cane 61
Relax into Balance: And You Can Stand Forever 67
Finding Your Gyroscope 71
The Fisherman 75
Afterword 79
Glossary 81
Bibliography 83

May the gift of tai chi connect you to a more complete life.

Foreword

Tai Chi has been called the Great Primordial Beginning. It is generated from Wu Chi, or the Ultimate Nothingness. Tai Chi is a moving power or dynamic state, the source of yin and yang. It is a philosophy from which principles, concepts, and beliefs have been derived.

In North America, the term tai chi has been mistakenly used to refer to not only the extensive philosophy of Tai Chi, but also a practice known as tai chi ch'uan, which is a form/dance that exercises the broader philosophical beliefs known as Tai Chi. The practice of tai chi ch'uan shares many of the tenets of its namesake. Both are represented by the universal curved circle symbolizing the idea of yin and yang and the interplay of complementary opposites. They share concepts found in Confucianism, Taoism, and Zen Buddhism such as the harmony of the yin and yang and the concept of the universe being a vast organism and the human body a small representation of it. The principles of continuity and of the circle are also a part of their shared understandings.

Lao Tsu states the following:
Mankind follows the ways of the earth,
The earth follows the ways of heaven,
Heaven follows the ways of Tao,
And Tao follows the ways of Nature.

What Lao Tsu is referring to as Nature embodies such concepts as Returning and Softness. Within the concept of Returning is the implication of movement. Implicit in movement is change, and Lao Tsu believes in a reversion to the original medium as a law of Nature.

The concept of Softness is also mentioned in Lao Tsu's Tao Te Ching . There is a reference to man being soft and supple when he is young and healthy and becoming hard and rigid at the time of his death. Lao Tsu states that the softest of things can defeat the hardest of things and draws an analogy to water and its traits and abilities. In regards to water, Lao Tsu's Tao Te Ching states the following;

Under Heaven nothing is more soft and yielding than water.

Yet for attacking the solid and strong, nothing is better.

It has no equal.

Tai chi ch'uan (also spelled taijiquan) germinates directly from the concepts of Tai Chi, whose seeds can be found in Tao Te Ching, and whose roots have been nourished by such works as T'ai Chi Classics and Zhang Sanfeng's Taijiquan Theory. There are many concepts that make up and define Tai Chi, and reading these three works will take you well beyond the few ideas I have already mentioned.

The mass public in the Occident have for years used the term tai chi for what is, in fact, tai chi ch'uan. I ask forgiveness from my readers for my use of the broader and more popular term tai chi in referring to both. By using the more encompassing term tai chi, I am referring not only to the broad philosophy of Tai Chi per se, but to the form of tai chi ch'uan as well. All concepts discussed are in agreement because neither contradicts the other.

Introduction

"Tai Chi alters both the way we relate to people and the way we process events of our lives." Arthur Rosenfeld

The practice of tai chi awakens a connection between the cosmos, the earth and man. An aroused inner spirit connects the mind and the body. Because tai chi is a moving meditation, it requires both the mind/heart and body to always be together in the present time, present place, and present activity. The core of a person's body becomes linked with the extremities. All movements begin in the feet, are developed in the legs, given direction by the waist, and expressed in the hands. There is no isolation of body parts in tai chi movement. The brain and spinal cord connect with the peripheral nervous system. The upper body and the lower body must be connected, and the inner body connected with the outer. In all this joining, the overall result is a unifying within man as well as the connection of man with Nature. The ever-present forces and cycles of Nature are interwoven in the movements. Stillness in one's motion and yin/yang manifest, becoming more easily felt. Within all this is an intelligence that predates all that is known.

The concepts of tai chi can provide a framework through which the world can be better understood and dealt with. Whether dealing with individuals or society as a whole, following the tai chi principles will provide a guide with roots based in ancient wisdom.

Tai chi is a gift that one can have for life. It requires no equipment and can be practiced anywhere in the world, whether it's on a mountaintop or a secluded beach, or in a spacious field or a small room—be it on a cruise ship or in the confines of a prison cell. Tai chi becomes something special that no one can take away from you. It captures and complements the moment.

In the following chapters I will attempt to show how tai chi is present in our everyday life—there only to be recognized, felt, and developed.

THE GIFT

The Gift

Making tai chi a way of life has always been an interest of mine, and it has always come naturally. I enjoy playing the forms and have always realized the power its principles offered.

Viewing the world through tai chi eyes, I realize the role tai chi can play in processing everything from sports to dance to medicine to the world of business and even to love and war.

Tai chi is a gift I was given by all my instructors and by destiny. Hopefully this book will open a door and create an exciting segue that others will discover.

Tai chi is about connections. In the world we live in today, many broken or disconnected lives can be made whole again. Without these needed connections, we are like a single hand trying to clap.

Probably the gift of tai chi I enjoy the most is its making possible a dance with nature. I have traveled to some beautiful and awe-inspiring parts of the world that I hungered to connect with. Tai chi has made that connection and offered me the opportunity to dance with the earth and the cosmos, my friends. When done with groups of people, a special energy is born and friendship is felt.

Yes, there is a martial aspect as well. Tai chi can serve you well in self-defense. Moving in a fast . . . slow . . . hard . . . soft manner makes it an effective and awesome method of defense. But one must keep in mind a Shaolin saying:

Weak Mind Weak Fist.

Strong Mind, No Need for Fist.

It would be a better world if all people received the Gift of Tai Chi.

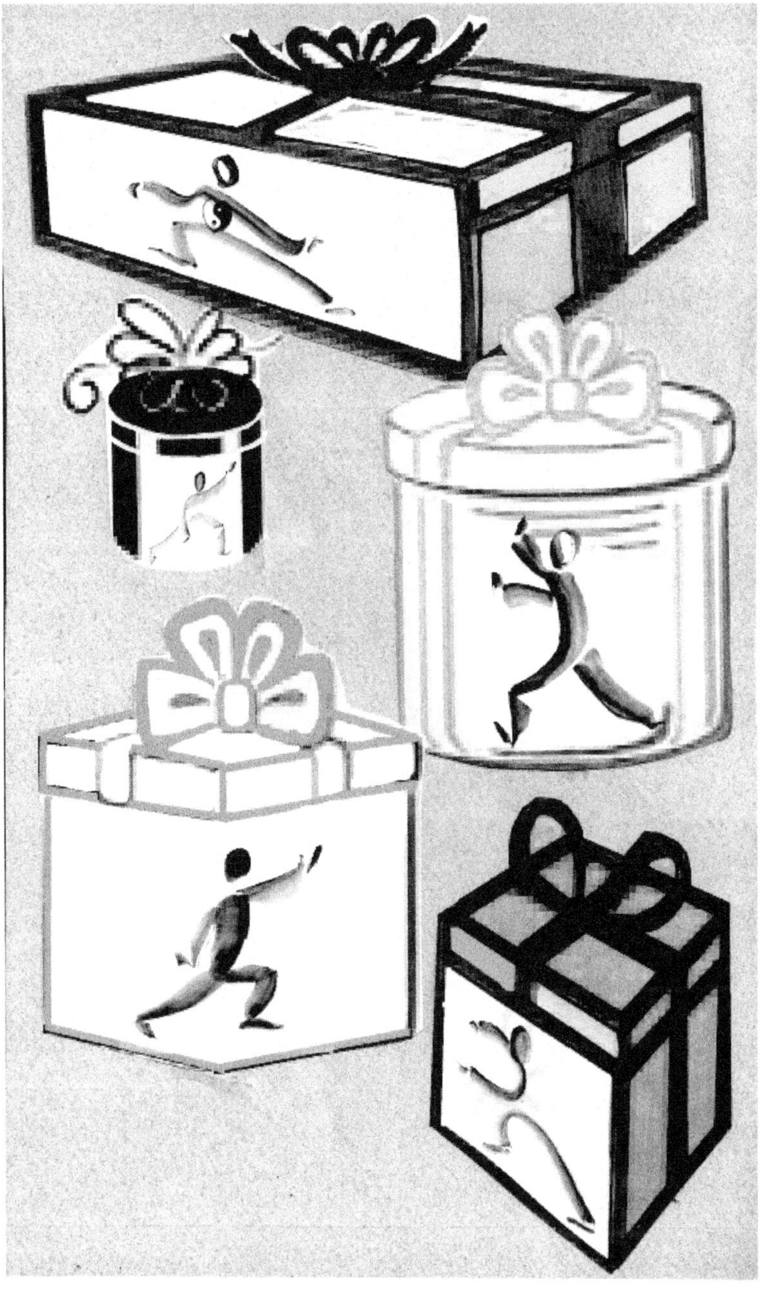

SHADOW TAI CHI

It was late November in the mountains of Colorado. My excitement was sparking as I chose my path under a clear blue sky fueled by a bright sun. Today's daily walk would be special—much longer than usual and into an area I had not traveled before. Scattered patches of snow remained on the fields from an earlier day.

The day's ever-present sun was just gorgeous. It occurred to me that perhaps nowhere else in the world does the sun have the quality that it has at seventy-five hundred feet. Because of that quality, a certain shadow is produced that can't be found anywhere else. One of the things I like to do in the mountains is watch my shadow, in case a mountain lion or some other creature comes up behind me unannounced. When walking through the fields and coming upon the occasional clump of spruce or taller pines, or the out-cropping of a massive boulder, I am reminded that the danger of a cat does exist, but actual sightings are rare. I have never come across one, nor do I seriously worry about doing so, but that doesn't mean one shouldn't be aware of the potential danger. My shadow really seemed powerful on this day, and it would be easy to see if anything was coming up from behind.

For the past few weeks I had noticed my shadow while doing tai chi outside in the fields. It had crisp edges that contributed to the flow of my movements. I thought it was special, but I just took enjoyment in my play without examining it further. Today, however, it became overpowering and evident that there was something almost sacred in the shadows. Could it truly be because of this sun at seventy-five hundred feet? It was an insight that was more of an intuition, something really, really hard to describe. The silhouette was not distorted. It was full and vibrant. I was in an open area and started some tai chi moves. Glancing down at my shadow, a flowing movement became magical. Within seconds I *became* the *flow*. I could see my flow in the shadow and feel it in my body and spirit. I felt an integration. After all, tai chi is about integrating, connecting your core with your extremities, the upper body with the lower body, the mind with the body, and the cosmos and world with one's self. It was all happening while watching my dark, unlit image against Mother Earth. As I was being transformed to another level by all of this, something began to happen: my Inner Shadow began to appear. Everybody has that yin side to their yang. There was a feeling I had never felt before. The external shadow seemed to be moving in a smoother flow than I could have ever thought possible. I even started to wonder if it was truly being created only by me. It had such a fluidity, and it awakened my Inner Shadow. The Inner Shadow is that side that we don't normally see or feel because it is usually the inactivated (insubstantial) aspect of us, perhaps reaching to our own DNA, but definitely into our subconscious or even into the unconscious.

Everybody has an Inner Shadow, and mine was now manifesting—becoming more substantial. When it is materialized, our *primitive* martial arts are called upon. That's when our primordial self is aroused to integrate with our known self to produce a martial artist unequaled.

My Inner Shadow was connecting to my shadow on the ground, in the grass. It was very special. An integrating process that was really felt—that is, I could become the power. There was no question.

So I began thinking, *Shadow tai chi. Yes! What a powerful concept! What a wonderful practice.*

In my experience I have witnessed some tai chi clubs' use of a mirror. Other clubs strongly forbid such use for a variety of reasons, one of which relates to the issue of vanity. These clubs believe too much attention is given to the ego in the mirror. Personally, I belong to a club in Denver that has no mirrors. Sometimes at night, my reflection can periodically be visible in the windows. It has sometimes led to a correction on my part, and I can appreciate the benefit.

Another club I was a member of in Boulder did have the benefit of a wall of mirrors. The mirrors were especially useful in showing what went on with the hands while the instructor's back faced the student during instruction. The mirrors could also be used to check if correct form was present. Almost never were they used to check flow and continuity of movement, which is the case with *shadow tai chi*. Also, when using a mirror, you focus on your arms, legs, or the position of your head, which can be helpful, but with the shadow you watch your body as one unit only. The shadow is one color and is a solid, single unit. Not so with the mirror's reflection. The shadow is one single unit that can reveal if a tai chi tenet is followed or not: When one part moves, all parts move. When one part stops, all parts stop.

As my walk was coming to its conclusion, I noticed a three-quarter moon in a steel blue late afternoon sky. I had walked a lot of vertical in my trip. Today was a day of connection and integration as I viewed the faint silver moon. The idea of a shadow and the Inner Shadow still stays with me, and it is something I now practice and call shadow tai chi.

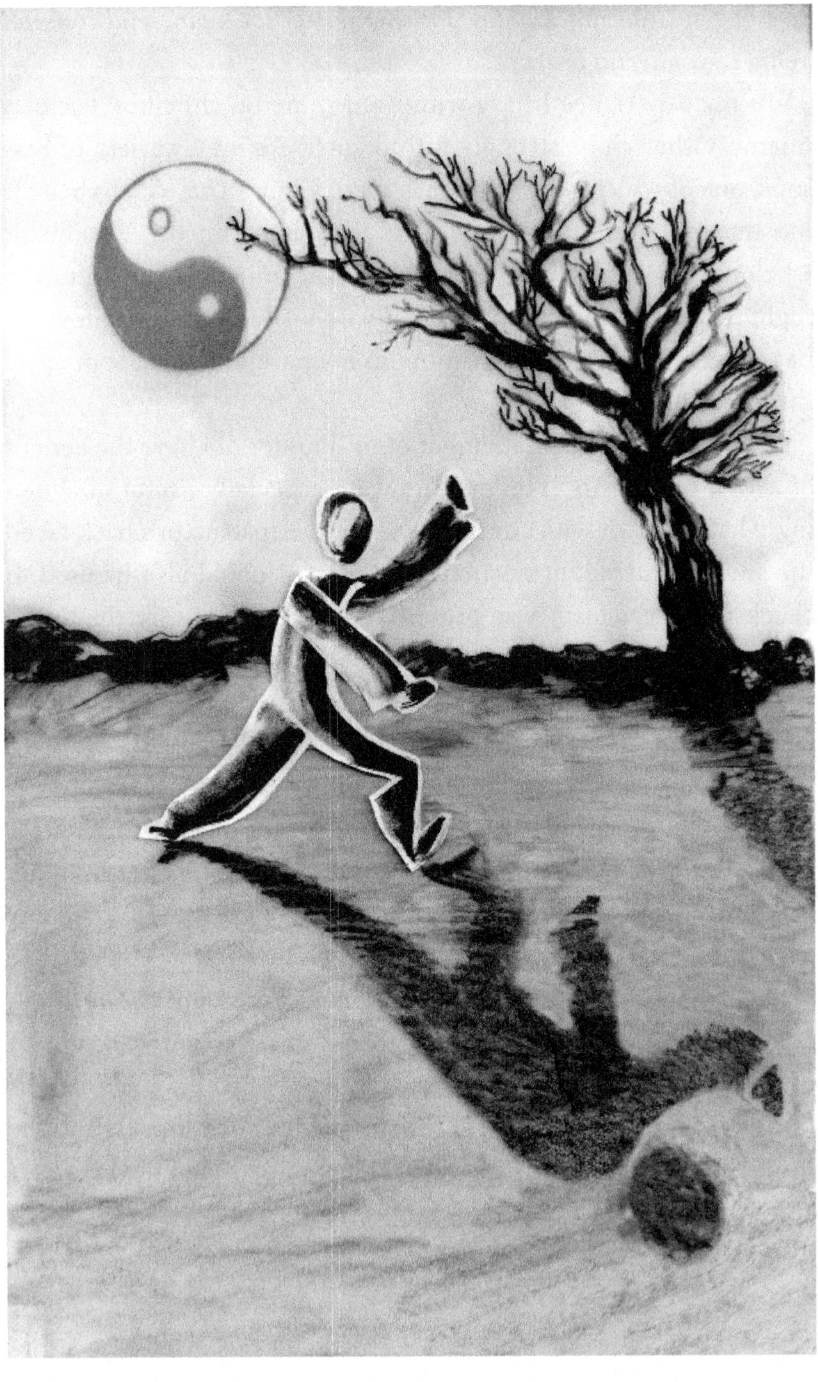

TAI CHI COMES TO A CHILD

Spring skiing is my favorite. Warm, sunny skies with fresh snow from cool nights are the ingredients that create lifelong memories. Such was the day I found myself descending the mountain, yelling instruction to my eight-year-old grandson. His father is a former ski instructor and wanted him to practice without the use of ski poles. My grandson was ahead of me, wanting to run full speed ahead with his ski tips pointing in a downhill direction.

"Stop, Caden!" I yelled, seeking a fresh chance to give much-needed advice.

A spray of snow filled the air as my skis carved into the hill in a sharp turn, stopping just uphill from the lad.

"I want you to learn how to make great turns," I said. "Can you make a series of turns going down the hill? Turn left, then right, left, then right. Can you show me some really nice turns?"

He looked in the downhill direction and without a word started skiing. I quickly was in pursuit.

"Look, Grandpa! Tai chi turns," he yelled back.

Momentarily not knowing what he was talking about, I skied wide and to his side to see why he was referring to these great turns as tai chi turns. A huge smile filled my face at what I saw. He was holding an imaginary ball with his right hand on top, left on the bottom, skiing to the left. As he transferred his weight from the right ski, his right foot became "empty" and his weight transferred to the left ski, carving a right turn while turning his imaginary ball over, sinking into the turn. Now he did the opposite and turned to the left, rolling the imaginary ball over again.

Yes, he was becoming the ball in his turns. Employing the principles of Substantial, or full, and Insubstantial, or empty, "empty," full, empty, full, turning like the ball. Yes! He had discovered, on his own, a personal tai chi form of skiing. This was something I had never taught him, and one only wonders how such ideas manifest. It was discovering something for the first time. A sort of natural outgrowth for him and a rebirth of sorts for me.

He was living tai chi. The Substantial, or fully weighted foot (yang side), was allowed to transfer back to the previously Insubstantial, empty foot (yin aspect). And so he went, back and forth, carving his tai chi curves and going with the flow.

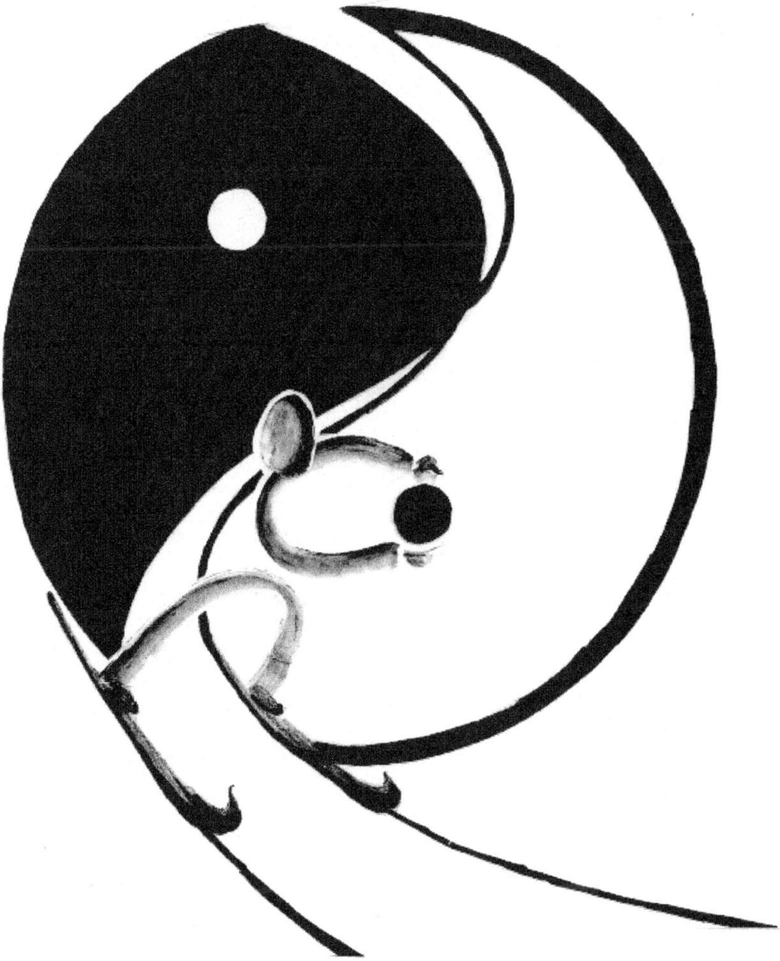

TAI CHI AND THE SEA

I am blessed to have not only lived in the mountains of Colorado but also in a cottage by the sea on Vancouver Island with my wife, who is also my tai chi partner. Thus our tai chi business name: Sea to Sky Tai Chi. It is very special to do tai chi in places with good energy, and when traveling to such places we never miss the opportunity to connect with nature. From one of the tea houses near Lake Louise (one has a beautiful waterfall, and both have a fulfilling cup of tea) to the beaches of Hawaii, Maine, and Vancouver Island, from the Red Rocks of Colorado to the desert beauty of the vortex of Sedona, Arizona, we never miss an opportunity to connect with Mother Earth's offerings.

Living on Vancouver Island in a waterfront home makes one especially aware of the enormous power of moving waves of water. Even when there is no wind or white caps and the sea is flat and seemingly still, there is always a yin/yang "intelligence" controlling it. For those who kayak, the nature of tides is well known. High and low tides occur twice in a twenty-four-hour period. There is something called a slack tide, which is when the tide is about to switch from high tide to low tide or vice versa. When this happens, all motion becomes stilled for the change. In tai chi this concept is known as the Still Point. The Still Point can be thought of as a point where the yang or yin aspect of the tai chi circle is no longer expanding or contracting. There is a reversion to its opposite by the aspect that was expanding. If a person uses their breathing as a model to understand this, the Still Point would be that time at which inhaling no longer happens and exhaling hasn't begun, or the point at which exhaling no longer happens and inhaling has not started. It is that point of change—empty, in perfect balance.

The greater twelve-hour cycle of the tide is made up of smaller yin/yang interplay complete with its own set of mini Still Points. I have used the smaller, more frequent pushing and pulling of the tide, whether moving out toward a low tide (yin) or expanding in toward shore (yang) with my Silk Reeling. Silk Reeling has a yin and yang component, and so does the tide. They share a mirroring relationship. I have gone mid-calf into the water on a beach and had fun feeling for and trying to coordinate the yin and yang of the water movement with the yin and yang of Silk Reeling. Such a practice can often take considerable time, and that is where one can witness stillness in motion—and motion in stillness. If possible, try to use a beach of clean, fine sand as opposed to a rocky bottom. One's bare feet can get a better feel with the movement of fine sand underneath. Feeling the sand move around your feet can increase the sensation.

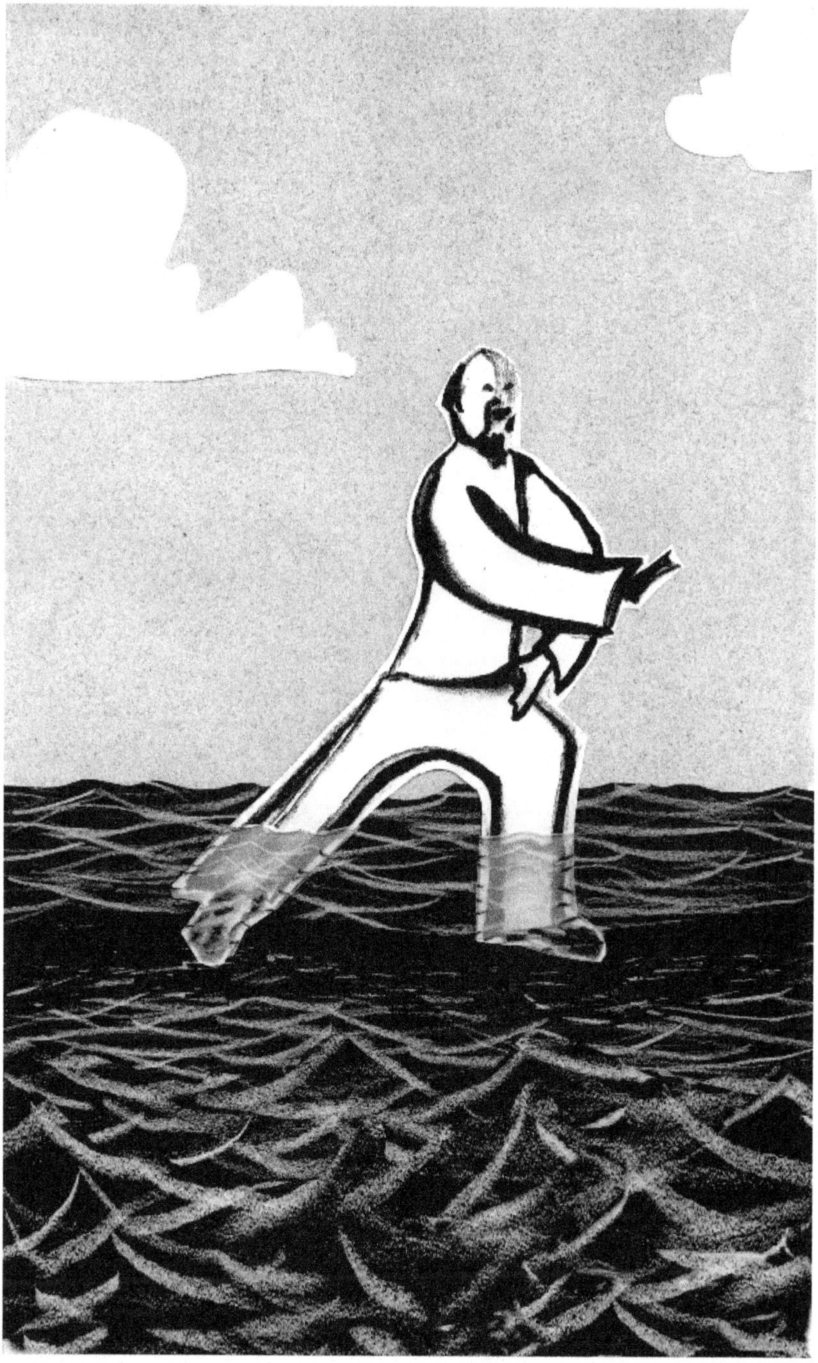

EMPTY SPACE

The other day I saw a store sign that had two letters missing in one of the words. My mind filled in the missing letters to complete the word, just the way Google fills in missing letters or words when doing a search. *So,* I thought, *it seems the mind is constantly trying to fill in spaces and add to my world.*

The Japanese concept of *ma* came to mind. Westerners, when coming into a room, tend to reference everything in relation to the objects in the room—a couch is followed by an end table, perhaps a TV or a few chairs, or tables with a vase. However, if the same room was viewed by someone versed in the Japanese concept of *ma*, their references would be totally different. Their observation of the room would be in terms of spaces, not objects. The space between these objects is what gets their primary attention rather than the objects themselves. They organize space, not objects. That is what accounts for the feng shui reflected in Japanese gardens. The beauty and simplicity of these gardens are overpowering.

Now, I wondered, when I observe tai chi instruction, how much do *I*, with my Western mind, *add* to the form? Do I add that which is, in fact, not really there? The adage "Less is more" came to mind.

And what about thinking in terms of space instead of objects? Could there be an answer to better my tai chi there?

After closely examining my form, I found extra things that were not part of the correct form. One thing that jumped out at me was my extra movement of the hands that felt good, but a simpler, purer motion was achieved by eliminating it. Somehow this extra bit was something that seemed to get added to the form over time. I corrected this by opening and closing my *qua* (groin) more in my turns and letting the hands and arms follow with *peng* energy in them. I recalibrated.

Constant self-evaluation allows one to recalibrate and return to the original instruction, removing that which wrongly gets added over time. One now removes that which he/she is not. When that is done, a better efficiency of movement can be accomplished. Employing the law of parsimony and using an economy and simplicity in our tai chi leads to more efficient movement and power. The mechanics of efficiency will be felt.

Following this practice and removing that which is not necessary helps me to feel xujing—a feeling of emptiness and tranquility.

In the words of Lao Tsu,

To obtain knowledge, add things every day.

To obtain wisdom, subtract things every day.

Next, I studied, by use of a wall mirror, the spaces between my arms and between my legs. It seems like forever that I have been studying my limbs and head and body. Now my attention focused on the spaces created by my structure. I found unevenness, and the balancing of spaces allowed for a more efficient movement.

I presently examine my everyday life looking for the unnecessary, which causes inefficiencies. Often, I also take this beyond the *physical* in getting rid of clutter: attitudes and beliefs are examined and either refined or eliminated.

At the mental functioning level, finding the space between words, sentences, and thoughts adds greater understanding and power to thinking—finding space in both the intangible as well as the physical. Eliminating unnecessary words that don't advance your thought sends your thinking in a new direction. Life becomes clearer and simpler, and a better connection is possible.

EMPTY
EMPTY SPACE
FOCUS ON THE EMPTY SPACE
SPACE
EMPTY
EMPTY SPACE
EMPTY SPACE
MA CONCEPT
FOCUS ON THE EMPTY SPACE · FOCUS ON THE
EMPTY SPACE
MA CONCEPT
EMP
FOCUS ON THE EMPTY SPACE · FOCUS ON THE EMPTY SPACE
FOCUS ON EMPTY
ON THE
EMPTY
SPACE
FOCUS ON
THE EM
SPACE
EMPTY
SPACE
FOCUS ON THE EMPTY SPACE
FOCUS EMPTY
FOCUS ON THE EMPTY SPACE
FOCUS ON THE EMPTY SPACE · FOCUS ON THE EM

THE SURPRISED THIEF IN BARCELONA

A translation from *Taijiquan Theory* by *Zhang Sanfeng*, as translated by *Yang Jwing-Ming, states:*

If yi (wisdom mind) wants to go upward, this implies considering downward. (This means) if (you) want to lift and defeat an opponent, you must first consider his root. When the opponent's root is broken, he will inevitably be defeated quickly and certainly.

A different translation by Waysun Liao states:

You should also follow the T'ai Chi principle of opposites: when you move upward, the mind must be aware of down; when moving forward, the mind also thinks of moving back; when shifting to the left side, the mind should simultaneously notice the right side---so that if the mind is going up, it is also going down. Such principles relate to T'ai Chi movement in the same way that uprooting an object, and thereby destroying its foundation, will make the object fall sooner.

The club members were gathering around a returning student. Greetings were exchanged and the conversation was filled with renewal. Other members found their place on the floor doing some tai chi moves as part of their warm up.

I wanted to extend my personal welcome to our returning fellow martial artist, and as I approached, joined the group surrounding her. Everyone was spellbound as the returning student began a tai chi tale she couldn't wait to share.

While sightseeing on a street in Barcelona, a large man grabbed at her purse, pulling its strap free from her shoulder. This 5'4" woman seemed no match for the man, who was a foot taller and outweighed her probably by a factor of two. Because of her tai chi training she remained calm and did not panic, not even with the difference in size between her and the would-be thief. She quickly realized that if she had just tried to yank the purse free, she would have been the loser in that contest, no doubt. Her training was ingrained, and without having to think, she let the man have his way with his pull while she was holding on to the purse. She was yielding, but rooted, while *sticking to* the object in question. Only when his pulling effort had totally overextended in a backward direction did she feel his complete loss of being rooted. At this point, she gave a hard strong push in a forward direction, making his already overextended pull even more exaggerated. Then, in an instant, she pulled in a reverse direction, toward herself. His unrooting was costly to him, causing him to almost fall over in the process. She broke the purse free from the thief's hands and fled into the street, running while holding on to the thing that held her most valuable possessions. For a brief moment she glanced over her shoulder and noticed the man in question had disappeared into the crowd. He had been defeated and should have felt ashamed . . . for more than one reason.

The practice of tai chi had saved her purse, filled with everything from credit cards to an iPhone. Her day and vacation were now restored. A sense of confidence and relief followed her through her remaining travel through the streets of Barcelona. She had not lost her root. Being connected to her root had enabled her to stay connected to her purse, and a new appreciation for tai chi filled her spirit.

Her story reminded me of when, as a young lad, I tried to uproot a sapling. I pulled and pulled . . . no luck. Only when I pushed the tree in toward the ground, hard and fast, followed by a sudden reverse upward pull, was I able to unearth the sapling from its rooting. This story reinforces what I now know: "If you want to extract something that is resistant, you must first *push* hard in that direction, and then *pull* with a rooted force."

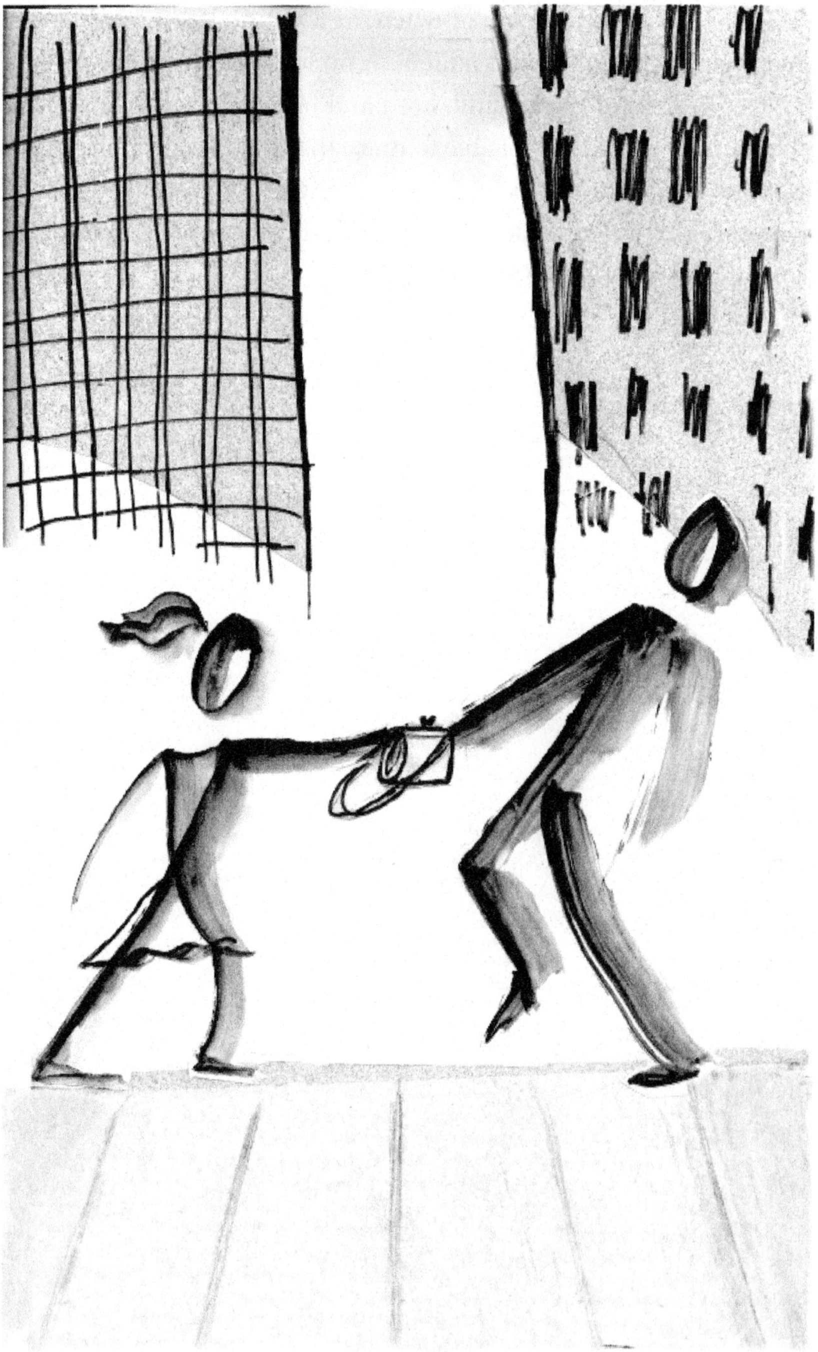

FINDING THE MUSIC UNDERNEATH

Usually once a week I like to work out on the machines in our local gym. I especially like rowing and using the leg machines.

The gym today was crowded and all the equipment was humming. More than halfway through my workout, I moved to the corner for some stretching because the workstation I wanted next was in use. As I glanced across the room, I noticed how many of the people working out were wearing earphones connected to a variety of devices. Wow, I wondered, are all these wired-up people connected or are they really *disconnected*? One woman was so into her music that I could actually hear what appeared to be music even though I was at least five feet away. Another man was watching a muted TV screen tuned to what appeared to be a financial channel. By the expression on his face, I knew where he was connected to ... and it wasn't his body or the activity he was performing. Boy, I thought, *are these people missing out!* Then I reflected for a moment and wondered if *I* perhaps was missing something. After all, didn't we use music in our tai chi group while doing the 24 Form? And music is often used in yoga as well as qigong. Dancers use music in their routines, and they are a connected group beyond question. So now I started examining why we use music in the 24 Form. For some, it seems to assist in the flow of things, but other members thought it a distraction. So why did we use it? The main purpose was to assist us (when doing it as a group) in knowing where to be in the routine. It is important not to go too fast or too slow—or worse yet, at an uneven and changing rate—while doing these forms together with sometimes as many as fifty people.

Days passed and the question hadn't really been resolved. I was in the high peaks of Colorado receiving instruction from my wudang master, and I knew he was one who could answer this for me. My instruction for this session was over, and the opportunity arose. Quickly structuring a question that would not sound dumb or silly, I asked how a person could know if he was moving too fast or slow in the form if he had no music or leader to gauge by. My shifu smiled with his eyes half closed, projecting an ancient wisdom. I felt like the kung fu character grasshopper as I waited for words of enlightenment. "By your breathing," was the answer. "If you breathe correctly, you will be at the proper pace. We will work on this."

My ride home was a long one. I now knew the answer to my question. *Yes*, I thought, *if I breathe correctly I will proceed at the proper rate of movement and fluidity. But what about the music?* I reflected and remembered what a former shifu had advised me, the words loudly coming into my mind: *find the music underneath.* Yes! That was it! I always wondered how to find the music underneath. Suddenly, I knew—by my breathing. Yes, that was the connection that I needed. And when that connection *is* made . . . from one's *body* comes the music of the universe. Tai chi tunes the body to the music of the universe.

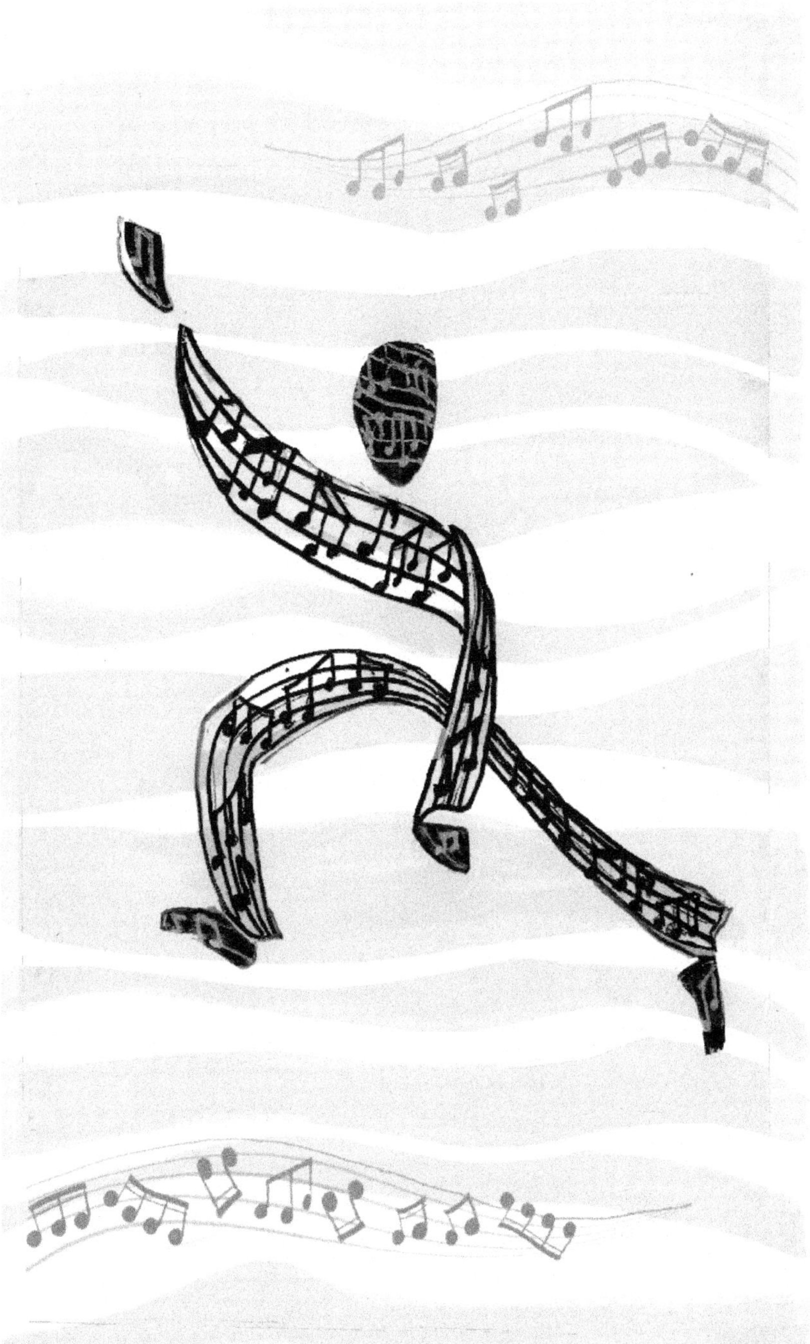

TALKING TO THE ANIMALS

"The mystery of life isn't a mystery to solve but a reality to experience." Frank Herbert

The morning sun had lifted the night's temperatures to perfection. By 8 a.m. a fresh, crisp mix of the night's leftover coolness and the new day's warmth was brewing. Two figures moved in cat-like motions on high, flat ground with the magnificence of snow-capped Mount Evans in the distance.

I was no more than ten minutes into my tai chi instruction when I glanced right to see a deer, hardly fifteen feet away. We continued practicing our tai chi walk. "Step like a cat, flow like water, stand like the mountain," I repeated as we worked on balance and strength.

Before long, two more deer were standing next to us. My student smiled and nodded her head in the direction of the deer. One of them even made a noise, almost like it wanted to engage us. They remained there for most of the lesson, and later my student said she could actually feel something when the deer were there.

The next week the same thing happened. This actually went on for months until the weather dictated that we move our class indoors. The deer became sort of our tai chi buddies, and we still talk about them.

Sometimes at night I would think about what had happened and wonder if something more was occurring during our weekly visits by the deer. The magpies often joined us without note, but these large animals were something special. *Hmm . . . I thought. Were they attracted because we were moving in animal-like movements, or could it be that they were attracted to us because of some sort of purity of state we were achieving during the tai chi?*

I reflected. The first thing that came to mind was that they might have picked up on our electromagnetic field. It is known that the heart, as it beats, produces an electromagnetic field five thousand times more powerful than that produced by the brain. From my readings, I also learned that the heart cells have a tendency to entrain, or synchronize, with one another. Along with this is an interchange of information. Could the deer's hearts be in synchronization with ours? There definitely seemed to be an interaction of two energy systems happening.

Our bodies have an innate intelligence that we will never totally understand. I, in time, realized that this mystery was not a mystery to be solved, but a reality to be experienced and appreciated.

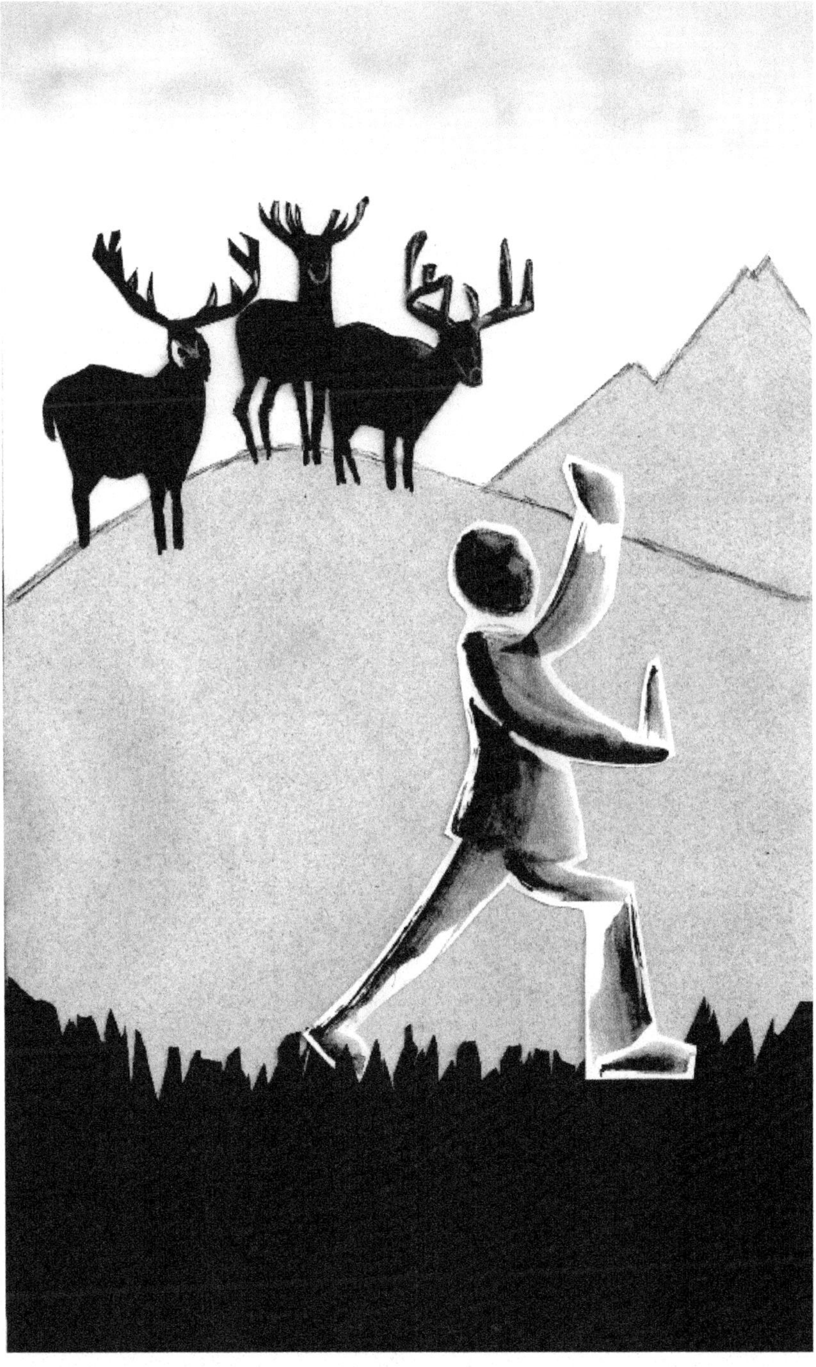

BEAUTIFUL HAWAII

Most fairy tales begin with the words "Once upon a time." My real-life fairy tale begins with the words "Once upon an island."

Once upon an island, two tai chi instructors rented a seaside cottage on a cliff overlooking the landing at Laupāhoehoe, Hawaii. The sleepy little town could easily be overlooked by the average tourist, but that's part of what makes it appealing to people seeking to unwind and unravel themselves from an overreaching world.

My wife and I quickly settled into our house on a cliff, with its large octagon window overlooking a lanai that opened to the landing at Laupāhoehoe below.

Doing tai chi there quickly became very special. Being surrounded by lush vegetation while inhaling rich ocean air and listening to the waves crashing on the rocks beneath gave us an appreciation for the magnificence of this island paradise.

No trip to the island, however, would be complete without a visit to Hilo, with its Liliuokalani Gardens and the masterful woman who does her "Water form" tai chi there. In this Japanese garden by the sea, filled with Zen sculptures, manicured shrubs, and a red bridge, moves a master whose movements flow like water, adding beauty and a sense of balance to the setting. In our two sessions with her, we received instruction for a qigong form which was new to us.

Places like the Liliuokalani Gardens have a power to inspire, and so it was one day when we were early for our tai chi/qigong instruction. A group of young girls was doing the hula on a grassy area just down from the small open building that is sometimes used for a cup of tea. Since we were early, we thought observing this might be a good way to use up our waiting time in a productive manner. It wasn't long before my wife noticed principles of tai chi being utilized. There was one tenet in particular that was overpoweringly present. To paraphrase *T'ai Chi Classics*:

The energy is rooted in the feet,

developed by the legs,

directed by the waist,

expressed in the fingers.

Yes, their energy was, in fact, rooted in their feet and developed in their legs. The circular motion of their hips and waists set the directions to which the energy followed. All of this was expressed in the girls' hypnotic movements of the hands and fingers. The direct correspondence between *T'ai Chi Classics* and these enchanting hula girls was powerfully displayed.

"Isn't it amazing how the principles of tai chi seem to be *everywhere?*" my wife asked.

I recalled a class we had given in Colorado a few weeks earlier. In that group we have a very accomplished violinist who came to me after class with a huge smile and raised eyebrows, bubbling over with great excitement. He couldn't wait to share a profound discovery he had made.

"We did two movements today that are exactly what I do when playing the violin," he blurted. Next he informed me how similar Cloud Hands and Silk Reeling are to playing the violin.

"It's not just a case of running one hand with bow over the strings," he told me.

I've seen various people do an impression of playing an air guitar, but never anything like what followed. The student held an imaginary violin and ran an imaginary bow over it. I had never had the privilege of hearing or seeing him play the violin, but watching him play this silent, imaginary instrument was moving. His feet were firmly planted and all efforts throughout his body were now being delivered to his hands. Upon finishing, he looked up to me, knowing that I understood.

"The movements are one and the same," he said with a sense of delight.

He told me how much he really enjoyed Silk Reeling and considered it hugely important in his life now.

Wow, I thought, *that's actually powerful. Tai chi is everywhere!*

Our last night in Laupāhoehoe was a moonlit one, and I went out onto the lanai. The full moon, along with the sound of the night's insects (*coqui*) and ocean waves crashing below added to a caressing trade wind. I found myself doing standing meditation—my mind, body, and activity all in unison with this beautiful place, which was made even more enjoyable through tai chi eyes.

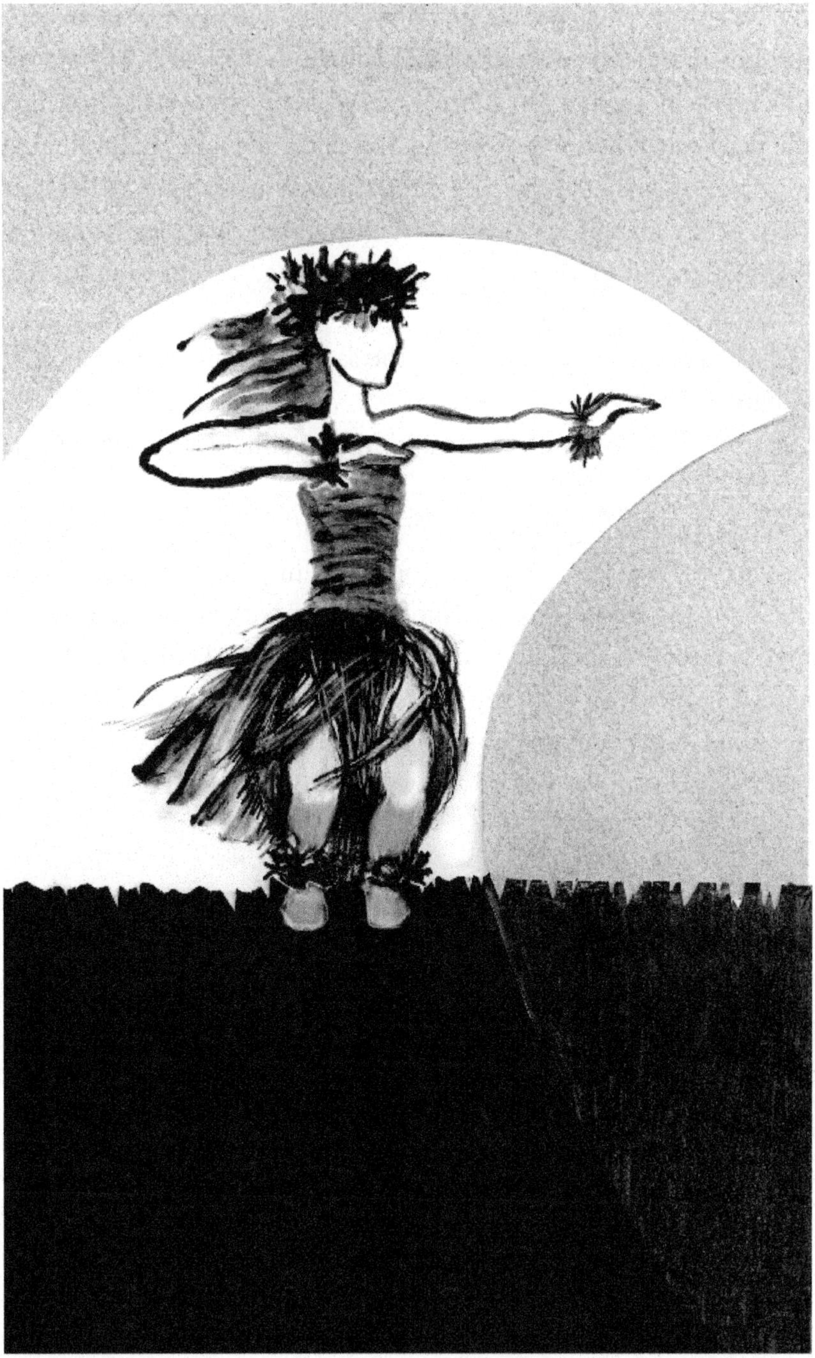

AS ABOVE . . . SO BELOW

On our last visit to the Big Island of Hawaii we were fortunate to have visited Mauna Kea, a dormant volcano. From the summit, my wife and I watched the sun set below what appeared to be the ocean but was, in fact, a somewhat different form of water. Fluffy white clouds extended to the horizon in a pillow of puffs, 13,796 feet above sea level. When measured from its ocean base, Mauna Kea is some 33,000 feet high, making it the tallest summit on earth—surpassing even Everest!

Because of its height, which places the cloud cover below its summit, and local legislation restricting lights at night, the area is virtually free of light pollution. To view the nighttime heavens with the naked eye or through a looking device places you in a different world. A special kinship was present because the night sky there feels like a home we were viewing for the first time since leaving.

Light pollution is not given very high importance in our world of environmental problems—the most talked about are water and air pollution. And rightly so—a lack of pure air is perhaps the most dangerous. Man has gone weeks without food and days without water, but try going more than five minutes without air, and we instantly realize that clean air must be present first if we want to live.

Far down on the list of pollution forms is light pollution, and yet it is one of the most pervasive. Not having a clear and unobstructed view of the nighttime heavens puts us out of touch with our cosmic beginning, replacing it with city lights and manmade stars. The fact that we are a microcosm of a larger macrocosm is lost, and we think of ourselves as something apart and unattached in any way. We lose our cosmic connection.

Some may ask if we even are related to what they envision as mere rock and dust floating in space, as we languish, existing in our own isolated world.

This all brings me back to a discussion in one of our tai chi classes in Bergen, Colorado.

When attempting to explain the concept of yin and yang in greater depth to our class, I referred to our lungs as the perfect example of yin and yang. When we inhale, our lungs expand and the air warms up—that is the yang aspect. When we exhale, there is contraction and the air cools—that is yin.

I next referred to the cosmos and talked about a similar *pulsation* that exists.

One of our students, who spent her life in science immediately volunteered, "That's called quasar."

"I guess you're right," I answered.

"So you can now easily see that the heavens breathe like us. They have a yang and yin aspect that is expressed as pulsations. We are a microcosm of the greater macrocosm. As above . . . so below."

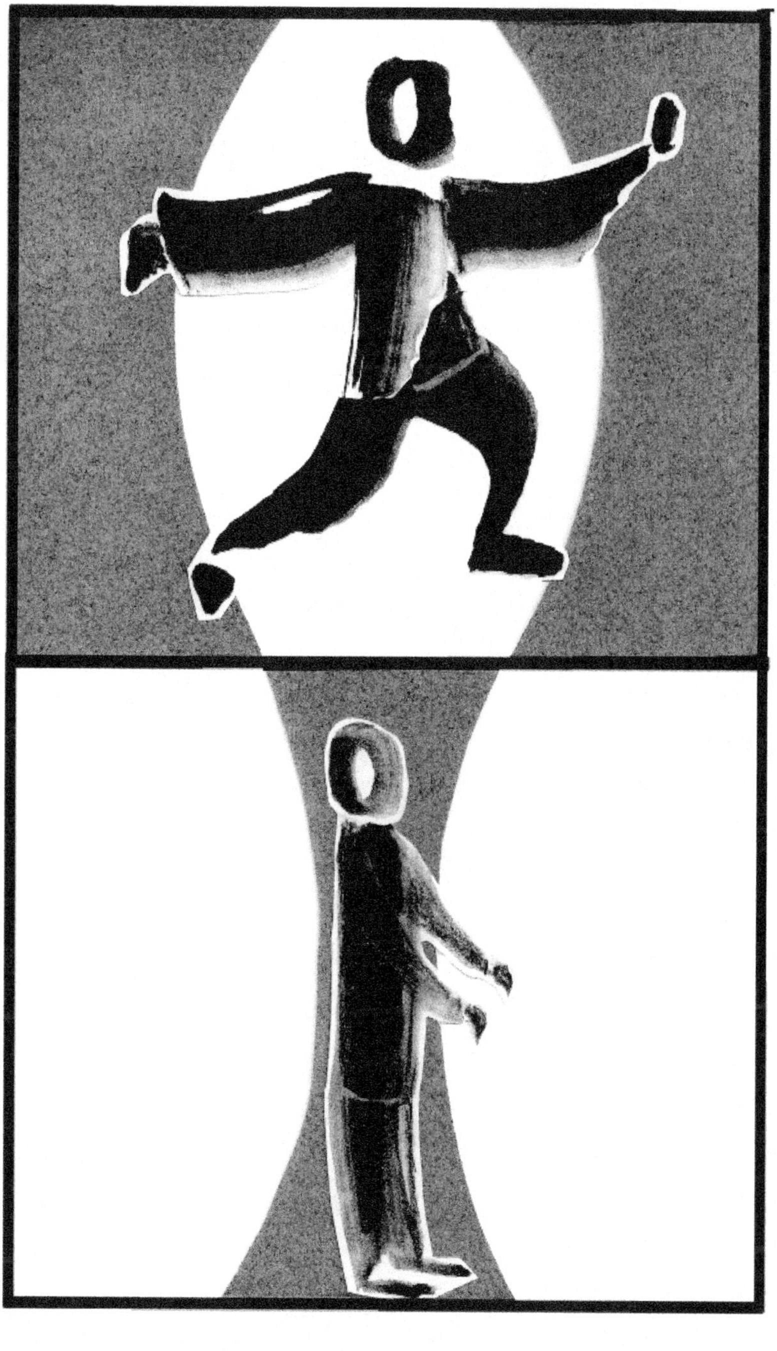

QIGONG VS. TAI CHI

The terms *tai chi* and *qigong* often confuse students. In a qigong class many years ago, I heard a student ask another, "What's the difference between qigong and tai chi?" The other student, having studied both, responded in a humorous way by saying, "They're both the same only tai chi is more fun." There were a few chuckles shared and the subject was dropped as the instructor entered the classroom.

I later thought about it and wondered how I would have answered that same question. Of course I have a good understanding of each, but when one has to put into words an answer, a search for the right verbiage starts, especially if you want to simplify it and use as few words as necessary while still providing a full and complete answer. I remembered the old Chinese lesson that a word is merely a finger pointing at the moon—it is not the actual moon, it is an intermediary and thus limited.

I soon realized how involved a task this could become. There are hundreds, possibly thousands of qigong forms, and tai chi also has many, many forms. To answer in a simple Zen way would certainly be a task. I personally favor the practice of qigong when seeking to build my immune system and turn to tai chi for developing balance and strength.

Years later, the concise answer came to me, like a gift, one morning after listening to a talk delivered by my wudang master. The

The Gift of Tai Chi

Daoist group had invited some new prospective students who had absolutely no training in this area. They were guests for this special day.

The lengthy talk ended and questions were open to the audience. The guests were sitting there fully saturated by all they had been introduced to. It seemed no one had any questions. The session appeared over until one of the guests, with a newfound smile, shot his hand up high, eagerly waiting to ask his question.

"What is the difference between qigong and tai chi?" he asked.

Oh no, I thought. *This is going to require a five-minute answer, not to mention that many aspects of each had just been covered by the master.* I cringed as I waited, expecting a rehashing of what had just been covered.

The master paused for a moment, and answered: "Tai chi is finding stillness in motion. Qigong is finding motion in stillness."

Wow, so few words, I thought, *but so powerful.*

On the way home, I couldn't stop thinking about his brief but complete answer. Yes, qigong and tai chi are two aspects of the same thing. Opposite but complementary. Motion is yang, stillness is yin. Yes again, after all . . . motion cannot control motion. An opposite force, stillness, must be present. And within the yin of stillness is the seed of its opposite.

That was the short explanation I had been hunting for. My wudang master had managed to distill the basic underlying concepts and make them understandable within the framework of yin and yang. Yes, an explanation employing the concept of yin and yang plus the simplicity of "less is more."

TAI CHI IS FINDING STILLNESS IN MOTION
QI GONG IS FINDING MOTION IN STILLNESS

WHEN IS IT MINE?

The last efforts of winter were feeble, unable to cool the moderately warm, caressing winds and the early morning sun. The amphitheater at Red Rocks, in the very early morning, is a place populated by athletes of all descriptions. Running and hopping the stone bleachers, pounding out push-ups, and doing stretches that ranged from the more familiar to the exotic, resembling yoga.

The Red Rocks Amphitheater, located just outside of Morrison, Colorado, is a world-class destination for people from all across the planet. And being only a fifteen-minute drive down the mountain from my home also makes Red Rocks one of my favorite places for early morning tai chi.

A frisky, rather strong wind embraced me this morning and made moving across the stone floor a little challenging. I found myself making adjustments, not fighting the wind but riding it more in the way a skydiver would—meandering somewhat, and changing how I fit into the framework of the form. I felt fantastic, the wind causing my silk tai chi pants to flutter, adding a powerful dynamic. It occurred to me that even the greatest of tai chi players probably never do the form the same way twice. No matter how exacting they are, adjustments for the wind, rain, ground, atmospheric conditions, and more must always call for a variation. And from person to person, differences in gender, bone structure, and health add an even larger generator of variations.

A tai chi player can learn by copying many forms and techniques, but there still must be an *organic* growth that comes from you.

The path to tai chi starts with finding a good *shifu*. He/she is your first instructor. Through a good *shifu* you can imitate the forms, receive the benefits of his/her observations, and receive the principles and knowledge passed down through generations. The tai chi student should also study the *Tao Te Ching*, *Tai Chi Classics*, and the *I Ching*. In addition, the most overlooked tai chi teacher is Nature, which is the basis of tai chi. At some point you have to go direct to the source and make that connection. One should invite the day, with its variations in weather, to share this event with you. And the final teacher is yourself. You must be connected in mind, body, and activity to your tai chi. At some point real organic growth must occur, not by imitating others, but by your own discovery.

Later that morning a TV show caught my interest. A profile of country singer Keith Urban was the featured story. He mentioned that when he goes on tour, he travels with over a dozen guitars. The commentator was baffled.

"Each one sounds different," he said.

Urban explained that he does this to stay fresh and keep the music vibrant, that the sound of each is a little different. In this same way, tai chi students should embrace the differences in weather. The weather is always different and makes the tai chi resonate with a fresh energy. Nature provides opportunity for such creativity. The form is the song and our body is the instrument. We can't change our body, but we can change the way we play it and embrace the differences in our surroundings.

Doing tai chi in different places, especially those with an inspiring nature, can touch your heart. When it does, there is a biochemical reaction that will affect your tai chi and help you in your *organic* growth, making your tai chi truly yours. When organic growth happens, experienced students find a renewed excitement in the practice.

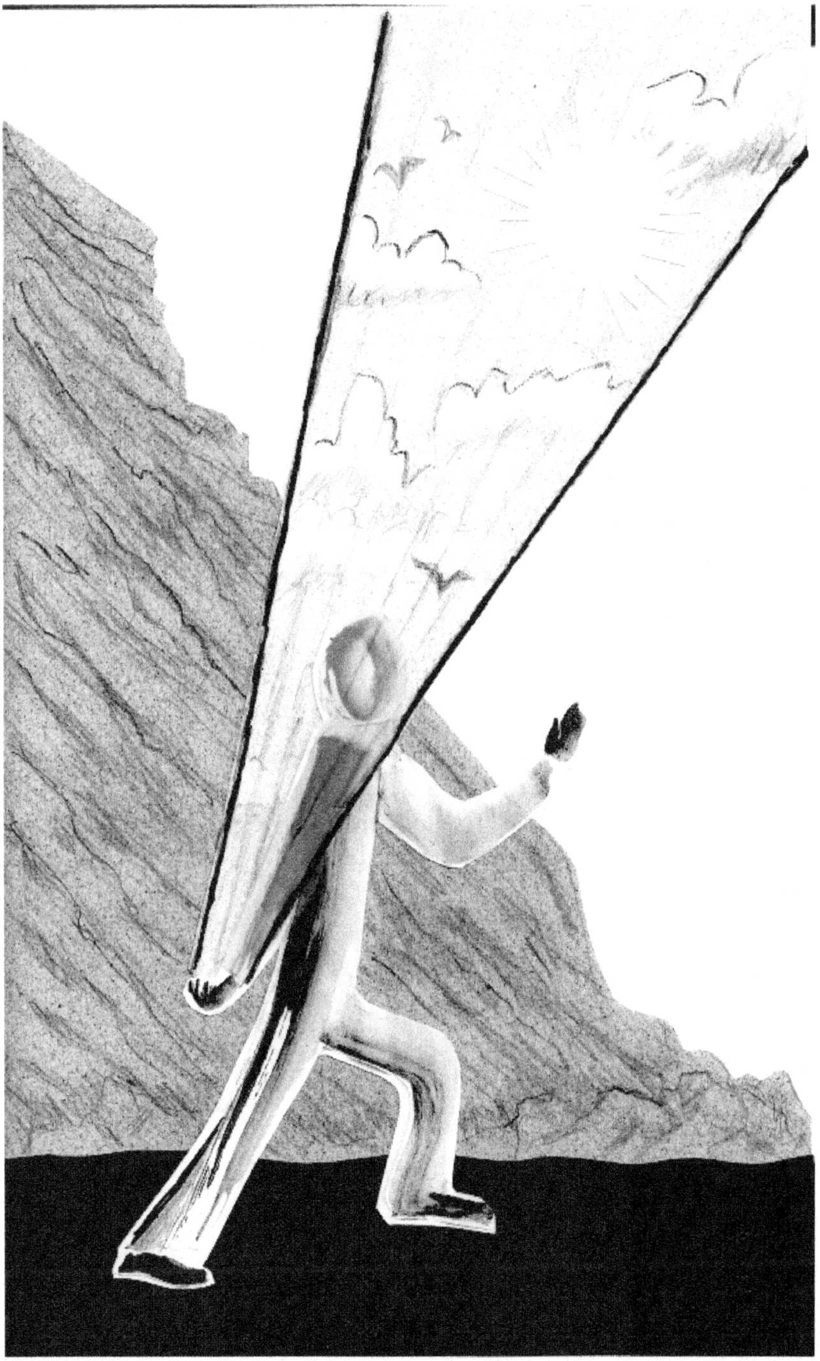

THE VORTEX AND OUR SPIRALING ENERGY

The earth's vortexes occur in areas of spiraling energy. They are located in recognized locations and account for the balancing of the earth's electromagnetic field. To the reiki practitioner, they would be likened to the chakras identified on humans.

A few years ago I attended a Jin Shin Jyutsu class in Oak Creek, Arizona. Most people might not know of Oak Creek, but close by is Sedona, and north of Oak Creek, just minutes away on Highway 179, is the Bell Rock Vortex.

Each day after class, my wife and I would drive out to the Bell Rock Vortex to do tai chi. The walk from the parking lot was not a long one, but an evening temperature of 108°F dictated that we take it slowly.

A vortex is a funnel shape created by whirling fluid or spiraling energy. All of the universe is a vortex, and our DNA mirrors the same spiral within us (as above . . . so below), as does the blood that moves through our bodies in a vortex circling around a vacuum center. One-third of the space occupying the bloodstream is a void accounting for the moving of our blood in our bodies, not like a stream but rather like a vortex. The heart's efforts are assisted by this phenomenon.

Spiraling energy is important in good tai chi. Eventually one advances from the up, down, and circular movements to a spiral.

Four of the eight energies in tai chi—*peng, liu, ji,* and *an*—can be combined in various ways to create the spiral.

In his book *Tai Chi, The Perfect Exercise,* Arthur Rosenfeld provides one of the best and simplest explanations of these four energies. He describes the four terms in relation to the center of the player's body. He identifies *peng* and *an* energies as using the vertical axis. Through the imagery of a bicycle wheel we hold onto the axles with each hand and place the valve of the wheel next to out breastbone. To start the *peng* movement, we spin the wheel first down so the air valve moves to the floor, then up, to be opposite from where it started. The first down then up and away path of the air valve is *peng*.

An energy is the opposite, but still a vertical movement. The air valve starts opposite from the breastbone of the person holding the imaginary wheel axle, the valve point on the wheel is spun first up, then down, arriving in the area next to the person's breastbone. So spinning the wheel first up, then down with the valve moving, inward, toward the person's breastbone, is *an* energy. *Liu* and *ji* energy are both on a horizontal plane as opposed to the *peng* and *an*, which are on a vertical plane. The difference is that the valve moves horizontally toward the practitioner in *liu* energy and horizontally away from the practitioner when *ji* energy is exercised.

Variations on these energies can now produce spiraling that is not only fun but also a beautiful dance to watch.

My wife, Linda, and I soon found ourselves doing the Yang 24 form at the Bell Rock Vortex. I asked her if she felt anything different.

"Yeah," she said. "I think I did, but it's not something I can find words for."

We next did a piece from the Yang 24 form called Ward-Off Grasp Sparrow's Tail. I chose this part because the four energies of *peng, liu, ji,* and *an* are all there. I knew how these energies were expected to feel and wanted to monitor any effect the vortex might have introduced. I listened to my body as my lower body moved energy in a downward then outward and upward vertical circle (*peng*). Next my energy moved in a horizontal backward direction (*liu*). Another horizontal circular movement moved the energy outward again (*ji*). Finally, a primarily upper body, circular movement. First moving upward, then inward and down (*an*).

1. *Peng* Energy (Ward Off)

The energy moves on a vertical axis, it first goes downward and then out and in an upward direction.

2. *Liu* (*Lu*) Energy (Roll Back)
The energy moves on a horizontal axis, rolling back and down.

3. *Ji* Energy (Press)
Moves on a horizontal axis, pushing in an outward direction.

4. *An* Energy (Push)
Moves on a vertical axis first upward, then inward and down.

That day's tai chi seemed especially powerful, and transformative, but just like in the case of my wife's experience, was nothing I could really put into words.

I don't know quite what I expected from this place considered sacred by many First Nations people, but my energy level was surprisingly high, especially for playing in a temperature of such extreme heat. I thought about what my medical qigong teacher from Vancouver Island once told the class when a student claimed not to be feeling the qi (although it had only been one month of practice at that point): "Qigong," he said, "is like a sheet of paper. Every day you practice, you add one sheet, insignificant and not even noticeable. But after many months, you have a ream of paper, very substantial and easily felt."

His point was that most *chronic* illnesses develop over long periods of time. They don't just happen in a week, month, or year. So the cure will also require the same period of time, and one must invest that same period in the cure as took place in the developing of such chronic illness.

So it is with most all of the Asian arts. The concept reminds me of a qigong form we use to do called The Slow Wind Blows (Feeds) the Fire. Those words always reminded me of patience and softness.

After my three days in Arizona, I wondered what my tai chi would feel like if I had the opportunity to play there every day for months, or even years. Would it become so powerful as to advance me to an unimagined level? I guess that question will have to go unanswered for now.

The Bell Rock Vortex—what a special place to do tai chi and connect with Nature, spiraling with the earth.

THE GOLFER

My only experience with the sport of golf consists of a physical education class taken while at St. Lawrence University back in the early sixties. The big 'breakthrough' in the sport at that time was an emphasis on attention to use of the forearms and keeping your eye on the ball. That was over fifty years ago. Golf, like all sports, has since evolved greatly, both in training methods and techniques. So it was with great surprise, last year, when a very good friend of mine who is an accomplished golfer asked me for some tips I might be willing to offer him for improving his game.

"Are you serious?" was my shocked response. "I don't play golf," I reminded him.

"Yes, but you practice and teach tai chi," he pointed out. "There must be some carryover from tai chi that can be applied to golf, no?"

"Well, let me give it a shot," I said. "From what very little I know about golf, just basing everything on what I know about tai chi, I'll give it a try."

I planted my feet shoulder width apart, or slightly more, facing an imaginary ball. I stood with my head suspended without tension or stiffness, dropped my elbows and shoulders, and relaxed my waist and hips. It is the *waist* that is responsible for bringing the torso, limbs, and the rest of the body to act in an integrated way.

Next, I allowed my tail bone to drop with soft knees, and felt the ground through my feet, remaining rooted. I could feel my energy spiral down my legs into my feet and return back up, further developing in my legs. My backswing began from my hips, turning them with my shoulders following in alignment. The arms followed, lifting the imaginary club. The swing came from my legs and hips as my shoulders followed, the arms and club following through, loaded with energy but merely following through to deliver the energy generated by the legs and directed by the hips. The shifting from empty to full in my left foot completed the movement.

"So," I said, "the actual swing starts from the the waist, spirals to the feet, is further developed in the legs as it spirals back upward, is given direction by the hips, and is expressed in the hands. The arms merely follow through. It's like doing a variation on the hula dance," I added with a boyish smile, somewhat confusing my friend who was searching for the connecting link to my analogy.

But he was impressed. His eyebrows lifted to make room for eyes that opened wider. "That's exactly what the latest teachings are," he said.

"Really?" I said.

"I guess golf is catching up to tai chi, which is many hundreds of years old," I joked.

It felt good knowing that tai chi principles had found their way into the sport of golf. I recalled how years ago I was told, as part of my golf instruction, that the forearms were the most important concern, and no real mention was made to hip and shoulder alignment.

The next day I thought some more about golf and tai chi and wondered if yet another connection could be made. I recalled some things I had read in Master Cheng's *Thirteen Chapters on T'ai Chi Ch'uan*. I wondered if this further application existed in his "Oral Transmissions, number 5, The Millstone Turns but the Mind Does Not." In this lesson, the millstone is a metaphor for the turning of the waist. The mind not turning is a reference to one's central equilibrium, which is a result of the qi (chi) sinking into the *dantian (tant'ian)*. The waist turns but the mind does not. When we sink our qi into our lower *dantian*, it acts as a gyroscope.

So, I thought, *the eyes can be on the ball throughout the movement, and with the sinking of qi into the waist (dantian area), a gyroscopic effect maintains balance throughout.*

Another part of Master Cheng's oral transmissions—Number 12, "Repelling a Thousand Pounds with Four Ounces"—might also be applied to the sport of golf. I like to think not of a push or pull of four ounces, but rather use the word direct. Four ounces can direct a thousand pounds. The example he uses involves the putting of a four-ounce rope, or in today's time even a fishing line, through the nose of a bull. With this in place, the bull can be led to the left or right. But the placement of the string is the crucial issue: if attached to the legs, tail, or neck, the same effect would not be the case.

I don't see why this analogy would only work in the physical sense; I think it could also be applied in a non-physical sense. I'm not sure exactly how much energy is delivered to a golf ball by a wood or iron in a swing, but according to my searches it's possibly as much as 2000 pounds. If we now think of a person's intention, or yi, as a small energy—four ounces in this metaphor—and it is placed in a strategic place—the golf ball—then it can lead the much greater energy/force in a direction of choice. Thus in our metaphor the intention on the ball is the four-ounce rope through the nose in Cheng's oral lesson, and the 1,000-pound bull is the force of the swinging club head being directed by yi, or intention.

Age-old principles are now being employed in modern sports. Yes, the Chinese are credited with the invention of the compass, paper, gunpowder, silk, noodles, porcelain, and paper money, just to name a few. So their contributions through tai chi should come as no surprise.

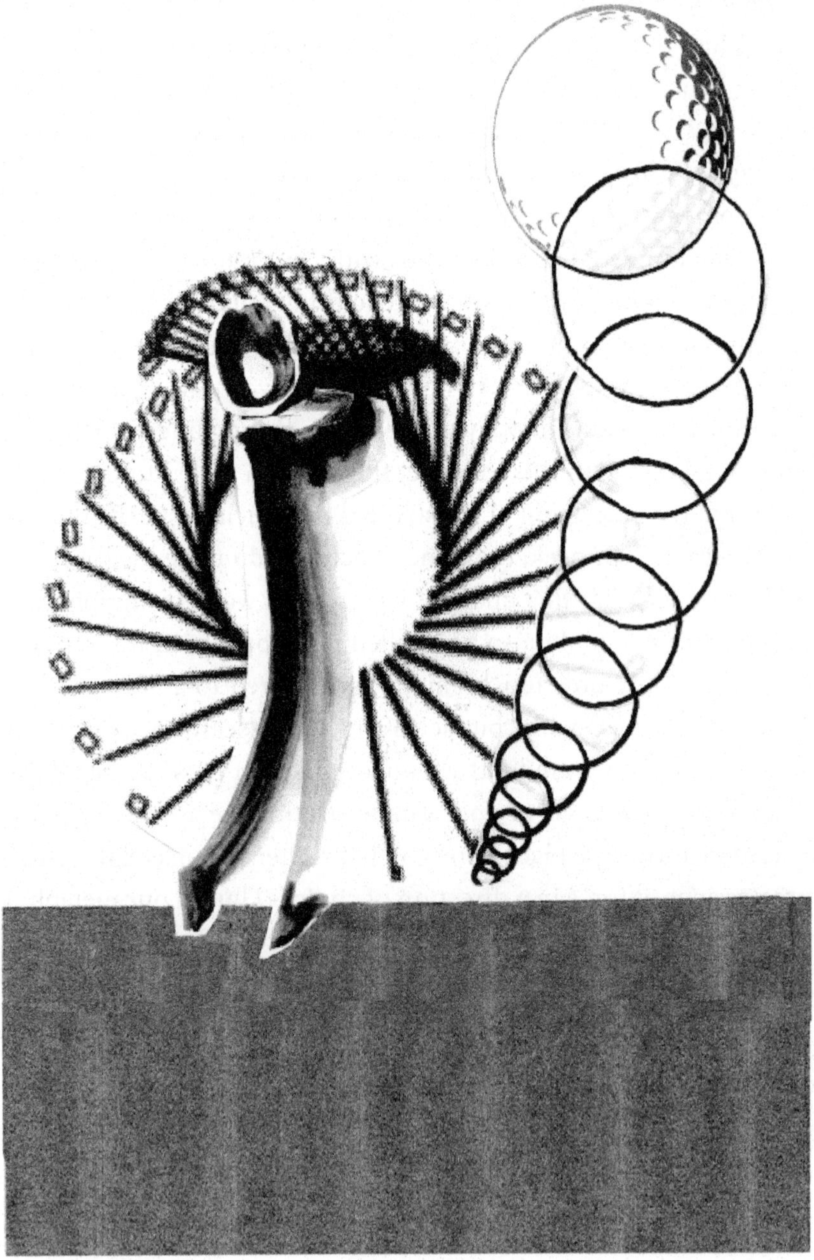

RAISING CANE

This chapter is not about the Brian De Palma psychological thriller or the David Carradine *Kung Fu* character Kwai Chang Caine, or about Caine and Abel, and it is not about sugarcane—that is, unless it is used to make a walking stick. No, this is literally about raising a cane.

The use of the cane in kung fu is more common than in tai chi. But a few people in the tai chi world are recognizing its potential. James Bouchard is creator of Beifang Qi Taiji Zhang. In his video he has flowing movements guiding his cane, carving lines through the air in creating his personal form of tai chi.

The cane has long been not only a fashion statement but also a stealth weapon that can surprise the uninitiated. Canes come in all varieties, some even as jewel-encrusted accessories carried by the well-dressed urban stroller. Probably the largest supplier of martial art canes in North America and definitely one of the leading promoters for use of the cane in exercise and defense is an outfit near Lake Tahoe known as Cane Masters. They have been a primary source of canes and training for me and have contributed to my interest in the cane in everyday use.

The most *common* use of the cane is in walking. Along with tai chi, walking is the other activity I do every day. Tai chi has been called the walking meditation, and the two are inseparable. For people who walk *every day*, there exists the risk that any possible "bad habits" of movement can be compounded. This is due to the fact that it is done so often, and because of the repetitive, unvaried movements that mindless walking can produce. To help with this problem, a number of books have been written regarding the subject. Two that come to mind are *Tai Chi Walking* by Robert Chuckrow and *ChiWalking* by Danny Dreyer and Katherine Dreyer. These books help you blend basic core principles of tai chi and qigong into your daily walk. But one of my favorite books on walking (though I believe it to be out of print) is *Power Walking* by Steve Reeves. Yes, this is the same Steve Reeves who was a Mr. Universe title holder and star of the *Hercules* movies. This book was copyrighted in 1982 but was ahead of its time in introducing some Eastern concepts to a Western world. Chapter 8, for example, is titled "Mobile Meditation" and discusses meditating, calming, and breathing.

One day I was receiving a Jin Shin Jyutsu treatment on a massage table and noticed that without the use of a pillow, I had a hard time getting the back of my head totally flat. Hmm...were my shoulders or back starting to get rounded? I reflected for a moment and the next day was observant during my walk. Going uphill, I noticed myself leaning into the hill. My shadow verified this. Something was going on in my walk and needed fixing.

Enter the cane!

I wondered if the cane could somehow be used to improve my changing posture. Most of the tai chi I do is open hand. Only on rare occasions do I use the sword, fan, or cane.

After much reflection and study of my evolving posture, I developed a routine involving the cane. First in a standing position, and then later I worked the positions into my actual walk. I tried different postures involving my cane in aligning my body. Three primary positions were developed: The first is the placing of the cane across my back with a hand on each end. This resembles a yoke across the shoulders without the two buckets of water that you many times see portrayed in prints and movies of Chinese people of old hauling water. This, I found, aligned my head, shoulder, and hips in tai chi fashion. The next two positions that offer me variety are holding one hand on one end of the cane while it is behind me, over my shoulder, and the opposite hand on the other end of the cane. First down the left side, then down the right side.

A word of caution: Everyone needs to devise his or her own use of the cane in walking. What works for me may not work for everyone. If anything you do hurts in any way, you should stop and not continue. Each person must find his or her own appropriate application when using a cane as an aid in walking.

The positioning of the cane in these various postures really has the potential, if done with care, to align the body and keep your eyes looking straight ahead, not on the road and missing the scenery. On the straightaways I merely carry the cane in an inverted position, switching arms for variety. Doing circular movements adds further variety. Sometimes I stop and do the aforementioned positions as a stretching exercise, and then continue my walk with my cane in hand.

Carrying a cane on your walk in the country, or anywhere, can also be helpful and reassuring if you need to distance yourself from an unfriendly dog or other animal that might want to get too close. A female friend shared the fact that she actually felt more protected from attacks when she goes for her walks in a park in one of the major cities where she lives. The cane has made her feel more safe and comfortable and has become her walking companion.

Since doing my variation of the walk, I have noticed my back and spine become greatly straighter. I even slept on a Japanese tatami mat with no pillow and actually felt comfortable. I'm now using the cane in various tai chi movements to challenge my balance and work on being centered.

Eventually I will probably not use the cane in walking every day because variety keeps a person fresh. Making adjustments and accommodating new situations is healthy. Remember that life is change. Follow the flow.

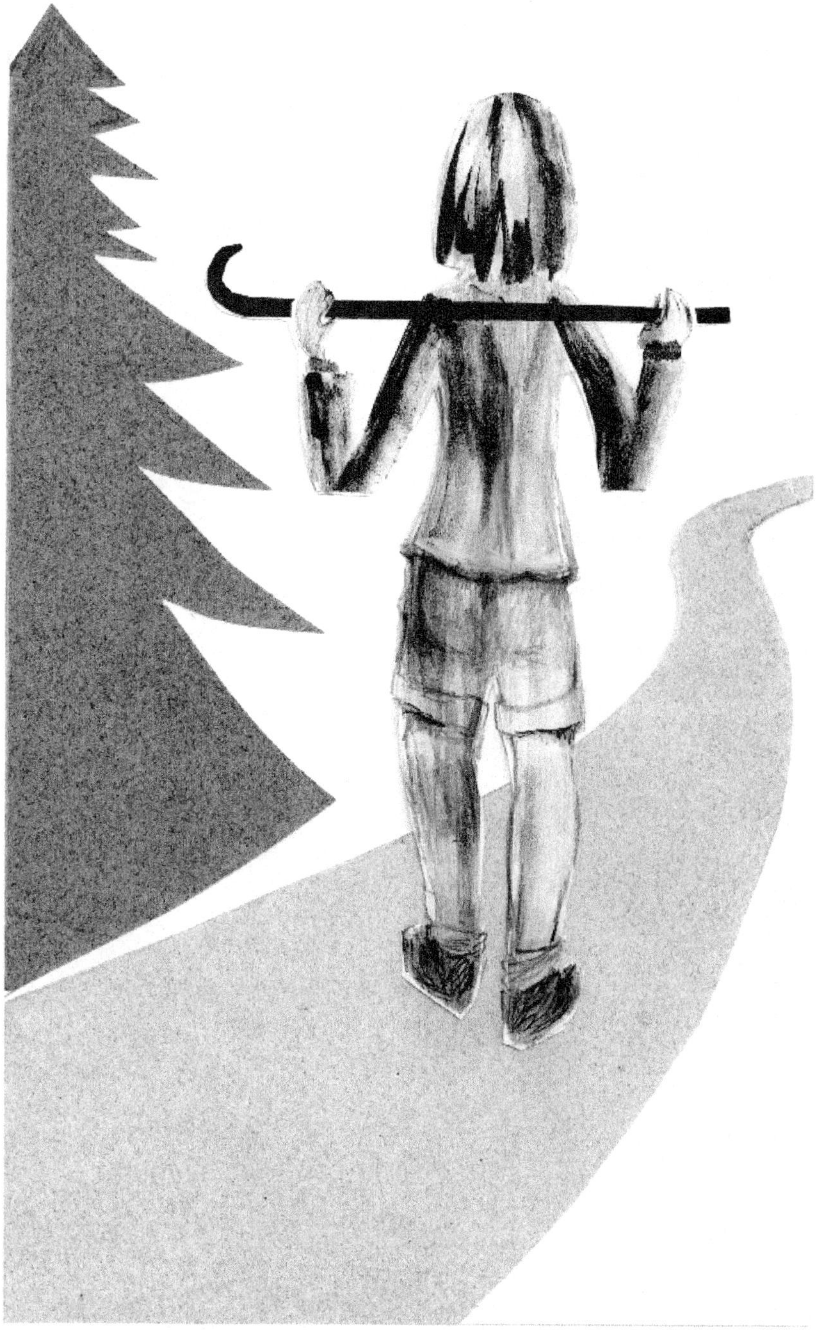

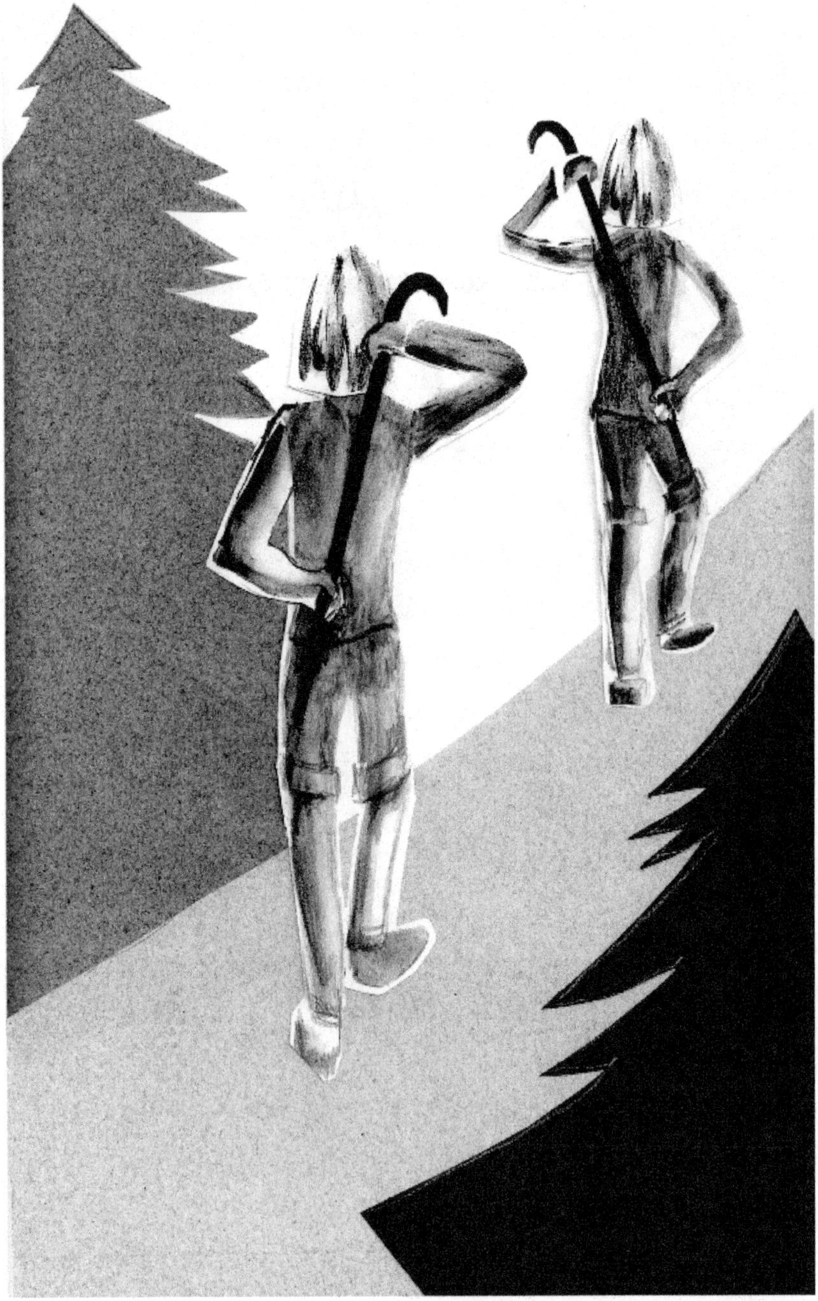

RELAX INTO BALANCE: AND YOU CAN STAND FOREVER

One day, too many items in my cart for the express lane put me behind three large shopping carts, each overflowing with provisions. I glanced at the other checkout aisles, which were just as backed up. Impatient people were scanning the other aisles in a constant search for a shorter wait, perhaps made possible by a quicker-moving line. Others were slouched over their carts or lost in their personal devices, perhaps texting or some other endeavor, losing themselves in the cloud. Most were trying to remove themselves from the present.

The lyrics to a song by the group Alabama passed through my mind:

I'm in a hurry to get things done.

Oh I rush and rush until life's no fun.

All I really gotta do is live and die.

But I'm in a hurry and don't know why.

Slow down, I thought.

Slouching requires more effort to maintain than good posture. That's because the incorrect posture now challenges your sense of balance, and you're constantly having to make adjustments. Also, for those people whose minds are in the cloud, not being in the present can leave you disconnected, thus *unrooted*.

Tai chi to the rescue.

For me, standing is even more comfortable than sitting, and that can be the case for any tai chi student who really understands the yin/yang aspects of the leg meridians.

The outside and back of the legs are involved with the yang aspect. It is what supports your weight and bone structure. The inside and front of the legs are primarily involved with the yin aspect.

People not versed in these Chinese concepts tend to rely on the yang aspect. That is, they place their weight on their heels and the outside edge of their feet. When this happens, we are using our bone structure as opposed to allowing our energy to make the proper connection by flowing freely to the floor. Putting the weight on the heel impedes the *qua*, or groin area. Your energy is blocked and not reaching the floor to connect. Soon you will be hurting and feel sore, which is your body registering a complaint. It's telling you, "Hey, this isn't working."

You must use the *qua* (inguinal crease) as a pathway in allowing your energy to drop. The energy needs to drop through the *qua* to the yin aspect of the leg meridians and flow down the inside and front of the legs. This is the way a true root is established. We need to take the pressure off our heel and outer foot and drop it all the way down the front and inside of a relaxed leg to the acupuncture point known as Kidney 1, or Bubbling Spring. Now the yang is not engaged and the yin meridians are. The energy is thus allowed to flow without meeting any resistance and flows in a spiral to the solid floor. The Bubbling Spring can only be reached by an open *qua*.

The upper body should have a relaxed waist. The head must be suspended and the arms and shoulders dropped. The center of gravity has to drop.

Remember the story of the sheet of paper becoming a ream. Time and practice must be ingredients in any endeavor seeking substantial results. Also remember the important role relaxation plays. A tai chi instructor on Vancouver Island used to come up to my wife and me and, in true Zen style, loved to share one of his favorite expressions:

Don't just stand there

Do nothing (No Thing).

Yes, relaxation is wonderful, but when you can do it while standing, it is truly intoxicating.

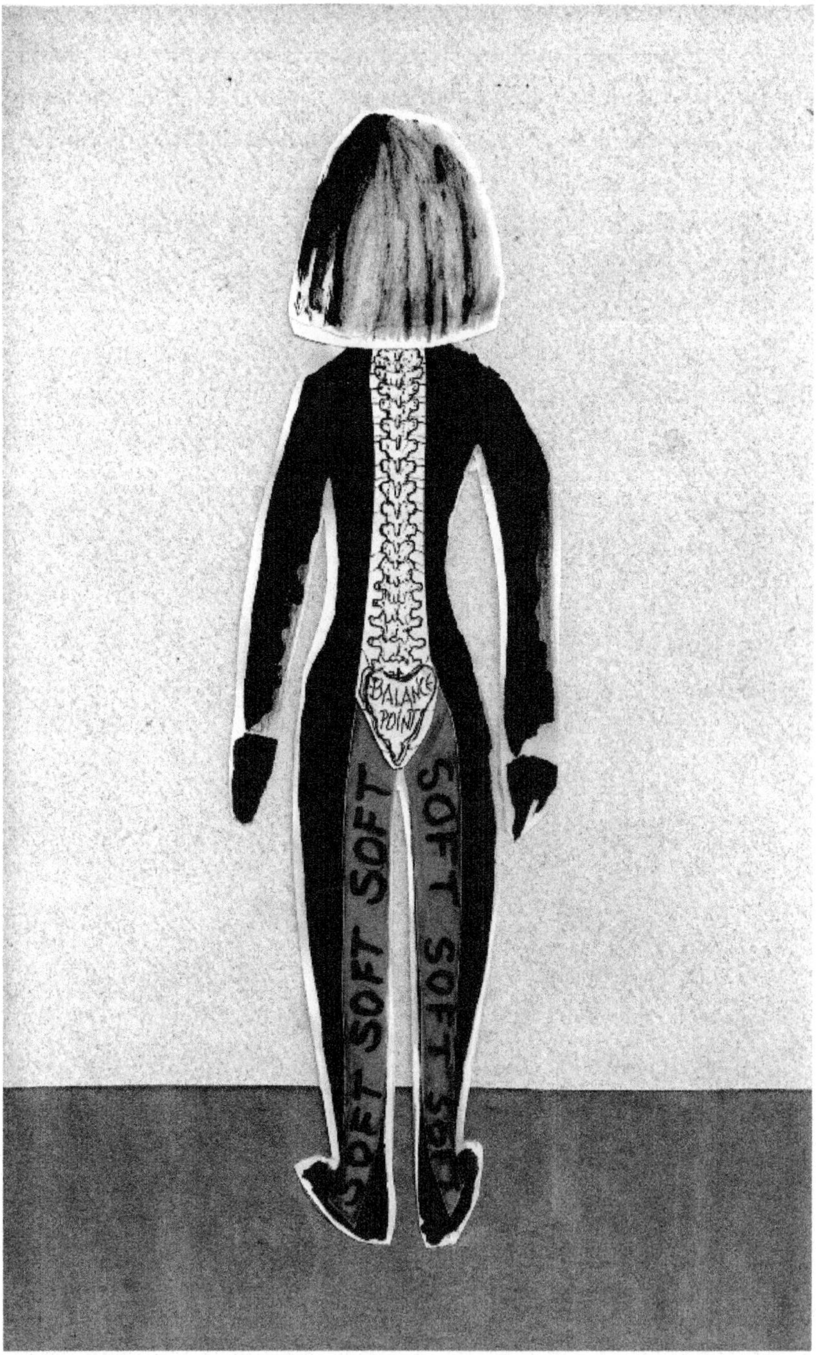
BALANCE POINT
SOFT SOFT SOFT SOFT
SOFT SOFT SOFT

FINDING YOUR GYROSCOPE

The spine is the most important bone in the body. It has twenty-four joints, and all the major organs are attached to it. The appendages and trunk are dependent on it for support, and its proper alignment is a requirement for good health. Thus we are always seeking the straight in the bent.

Finding that desired posture in a standing position *is* possible when doing standing pole (zhan zhuang) or meditation. It is also evident in the moving meditation of tai chi. But finding such form in the sitting position is often much more of a challenge, especially if movement is necessitated by activities such as typing or operating a machine.

A slouching figure is not only unattractive but can generate myriad illnesses, everything from curvature of the spine to spinal stenosis, and can have a negative effect on our organs.

A tai chi principle based on Yang Ch'eng-fu's oral teachings can help us in our enigma. "It is forbidden to use strength." Yang encourages one to relax, without using strength, and proceed from total softness. So that is our starting point.

Energy is the helper we need, and that issues from the sinews, unlike force which is dependent on the bones. It becomes almost counterintuitive, because we should *not* think in terms of bone (or the spine itself), because force is not what we need to work with. We must work with the energy. Qi has the strength of flexible power.

Drop the shoulders and elbows, suspend the head with the chin slightly tucked, allow the tailbone to drop, and use your *mind* to move the *qi*. The *qi* will move the *body*.

Achieving a straight spine while seated is only half the battle. If no movement is now required, all is fine. However, most seated people do arm movements and activities that threaten the newly accomplished alignment.

Once the straight spine is established, your body can come to the rescue. It has everything it needs to overcome your movements and still maintain the stability and equilibrium required at this point to maintain the straight spine. But it requires a little help from you.

The equilibrium we've established is not static, as one may think, but rather one that needs to not lose the timely responses to various conditions. We must not lose our central equilibrium. This is accomplished by inhaling to the lower *dantian* in a long, calm, and slow manner. The lower *dantian* is approximately 1.3 inches below the navel (2.5 cun/tsun). Keep the mind there as well.

Remember *Master Cheng's Thirteen Chapters On Tai Chi Ch'tian*? In Chapter 13, oral transmission 5 states: "The millstone turns but the mind does not turn." Remember that the turning of the millstone is a metaphor for the waist. And the mind not turning is the central equilibrium resulting from sinking the qi into the lower *dantian*. Therefore, the waist turns, but the mind does not turn. Thus when we sink our qi into our lower *dantian*, it, in effect, acts as a gyroscope.

It was a pleasant experience one day when a friend announced to me that she had had her "moment of intoxication." After trying the aforementioned suggestion, she was swept away by the effect of it working for her.

After sixty-one years of struggling with her posture, she field-tested this concept and was elated at arriving at good posture after all these years.

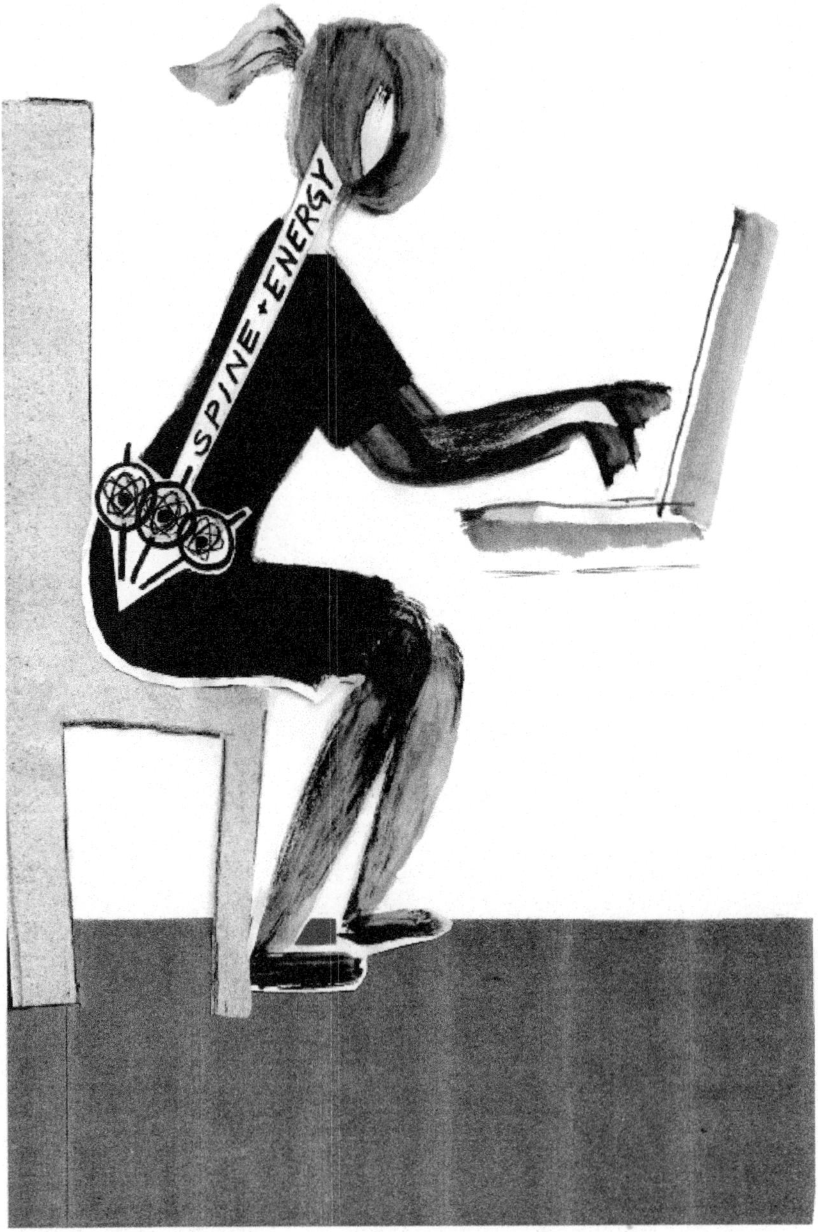
SPINE + ENERGY

THE FISHERMAN

I arrived a half hour early at the bookstore in Boulder. It had been a long drive from our mountain home, but I always leave myself extra time, eliminating any potential stress created by the possibility of unplanned delays. I was registered for a class entitled "How to Sell Your Book." A long staircase with a landing dividing the climb led me to the back of a room where a conference table accommodated nine chairs. *Hmm . . .* I thought, *I guess there won't be too many taking this class.* The next fifteen minutes passed quickly, and soon there were five of us at the conference table, brimming with an excitement, the type found when you think you are about to be told some sort of secret that can alter your life.

A lot of small talk transpired—the usual, where the speaker tells you something about himself and asks about your writings. A half hour of this passed without any sort of sparking occurring. *Wow,* I thought, *this is a bit disappointing.*

The speaker had been talking with the man next to me for several minutes when he paused, leaving a full silence hanging between everyone. He then looked me in the eye and asked, "Are you a fisherman?"

Huh? I thought. *Why would he ask me that?*

"No," I answered.

Silence again passed over the table like a fog.

Our eyes interlocked, and he knew I was asking why.

The Gift of Tai Chi

"You look like a fisherman," he said.

"I'm a tai chi instructor. That's what my book is about," I added, knowing that we had already discussed this.

In a flash I did a self-assessment before continuing. I was wearing a baseball cap and was dressed in clothes that might be described as preppy.

"Oh, I get it, I'm supposed to look like a tai chi man . . . right?"

He nodded.

I now felt challenged to the point that I needed to set him straight while still trying to understand any and all inferences made by his implication.

"Well, I'm not Asian, although my mother did have high cheekbones," I retorted, trying to establish some humor for balance.

The speaker turned to another writer and left me hanging with this unfinished problem.

It was a long ride home, and my emotions ran the gambit. I felt I had wasted my $40 fee for a class that offered me nothing! An intense self-inspection followed. I tried to picture my appearance. *Hmm . . . I'm not a fisherman.*

The point he was making, and I picked it up pretty quickly, was that I don't *look* like what he pictured a tai chi person looking like. So I thought, *Well, what does a tai chi person look like?* All my former *shifus* were Asian. So how can I look Asian? I can't change that. I thought of the actor David Carradine and what he looked like in his kung fu series. So maybe I should either shave my head or let my silver hair grow to shoulder length.

Wait a minute. Was his comment a valid criticism? I didn't look like a tai chi instructor to him, but is it important to look like a tai chi instructor to sell a book, or is it more important to *act* like one? Or better yet, just *be* one? Well . . . I think I'm grounded, rooted, connected in all ways. That to me is what makes a tai chi person.

How much credibility should we give to appearance? Is that everything or even anything? This interaction and subsequent reflection reminded me that you really have to be the ball, not just look like one. You have to be the tai chi. I guess looking the part could be relevant, but if you have five different people look at a person, you'll get five different opinions. So it's your actions that should define you.

Looking back on the class, I knew I was the tai chi person because I was connected. It goes beyond appearance—of course. It goes beyond what you do for a living. It gets far more personal than that. It's about being connected. You could be a cook, a teacher, a mechanic, a lawyer, a business person, and be a practitioner of tai chi. It is something that he/she is. It is being connected—his/her mind to his/her body. Being the connection between the cosmos and earth . . . being the human.

I am reminded of two giants in the business world.

Jack Ma, a Chinese business magnate and founder of the company Alibaba.com is a player of tai chi. He is a well-groomed businessman dressed in ordinary clothes. When he is in his everyday activities, he certainly looks like a businessman, not the tai chi practitioner he truly is.

And Guo Guangchang is the billionaire co-founder of the Chinese company Fosun International. He is a smartly dressed businessman who wears a fine suit most of the day until he does his tai chi in his silks. His tai chi is beautiful, a joy to watch.

Neither of these men look like tai chi people in the martial arts movies, but rather like the businessmen they are. But, the truth be known, they are tai chi masters both in their form and in their business dealings.

So . . . it's not about appearance—that's fraudulent.

By the time I got home, I realized what was important to me. Looking the part might sell books, but being the part is what such books are about.

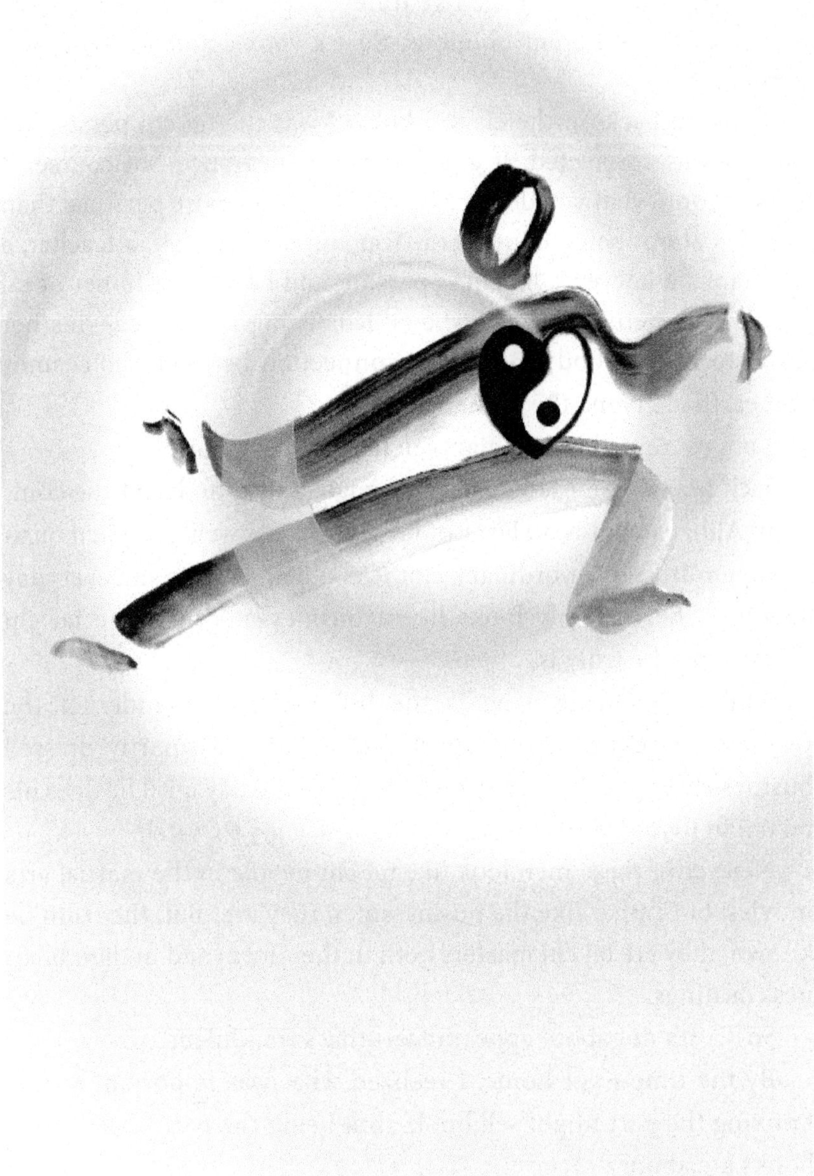

AFTERWORD

By practicing tai chi daily we connect with nature or what some refer to as the Tao. This is a connection mankind is finding more difficult to maintain as we lose our roots in ancient wisdom and instead seek the "cloud" made by man. We have used the yin/yang principle in binary math but have left out an important part of tai chi theory: the concept of connection and viewing things as a whole. Our research looks most times at isolated phenomena just the same way we isolate muscle groups in physical training, forgetting that the body functions and moves as an integrated unit. Remember the hula girls I mentioned earlier? Even the slightest movement of the hands or fingers originates in the feet, flows through the legs, hips, spine, shoulders, elbows, and wrists and is finally expressed in the fingers. There is no isolation in tai chi, just total integration connecting you with the earth.

Within water and plants is an age-old wisdom and knowledge. For thousands of years, people have talked of sacred and blessed water, and the plants have given us life by providing food and oxygen. The plants have, in effect, provided a means for us to "eat of the sun." This was all provided without us needing to do anything.

Many great thinkers in the occident have recognized the importance of our relationship with Nature. One of my favorites is Carl Jung. He said:

Our task is not to return to Nature

In the manner of Rousseau,
but to find the Natural man again.

Tai chi has affected the way I relate to my world. Everything from trading stocks to the weather is now viewed with the wisdom of Nature that I am connected to through the gift of tai chi. There isn't a day that goes by now that isn't altered by my tai chi gift.

GLOSSARY

Cloud Hands—A movement in tai chi in which one's hands mirror each other, moving across in the same sideways direction. Then the hands turn and switch position with one another and move together in the opposite direction. One is moving in a clockwise direction while the other moves in a counterclockwise direction.

player—The name assigned to a tai chi practitioner. Someone who practices tai chi.

qi/chi—Life or vital energy.

qigong—The practice of accumulating, refining, and moving qi. It consists of three components: Posture, Breathing, and Meditation. Can be either Static or Dynamic.

qua—A body section known to Westerners as the groin. There is a corresponding *qua* in the area of the armpits.

shifu—Chinese word for "master." It also implies "father."

Silk Reeling—The practice in tai chi that involves the rotation of one's body (cocoon) while the hands do a spiral action (pulling silk). The silk (chi/qi) is pulled from the cocoon. If one pulls too hard the silk will break, if not hard enough, the silk will snag. Thus continuity of movement and smoothness is developed to a high degree.

sticking to—Staying connected by touch to a person. One can also be connected to something in terms of their mind. There is no pushing or pulling action, just a following motion in the attempt to stay connected.

taijiquan/tai chi ch'uan—The interplay of yin and yang. Finding stillness in motion.

yin and yang—Opposite aspects of the same things that are complementary.

BIBLIOGRAPHY

Most ideas and thoughts, even when they are believed to be truly organic, are the result of previous exposures and experiences. The following readings have become interwoven with my personal experiences and contribute to my tai chi and the writing of this book.

Barrett, Rick. *Taijiquan: Through the Western Gate*. Berkeley, CA: Blue Snake Books/Frog Ltd. Books, 2006.

Bond, Joey. *See Man Jump . . . See God Fall: Tai Chi vs. Technology*. San Diego, CA: ProMotion Publishing, 1997.

Buhner, Stephen Harrod. *The Secret Teachings of Plants*. Rochester, VT: Bear & Company, 2004.

Chuckrow, Robert. *Tai Chi Walking*. Boston, MA: YMAA Publication Center, 2002.

Dreyer, Danny, and Katherine Dreyer. *Chi Walking*. New York: Simon & Schuster, 2006.

Huang, Al. *Embrace Tiger, Return to Mountain*. Berkeley, CA: Celestial Arts, 1987.

Huang, Wen-Shan. *Fundamentals of Tai Chi Ch'uan*. Hong Kong: South Sky Book Company, 1973.

Kauskas, Jan. *Laoshi*. Santa Fe: Via Media, 2014.

Liao, Waysun. *T'ai Chi Classics*. Boston, MA: Shambhala Publishing, 1990.

Man-ch'ing, Cheng. Lao-Tzu: *"My Words Are Very Easy to Understand."* Berkeley, CA: North Atlantic Books, 1971.

Man-ch'ing, Cheng. *Master Cheng's Thirteen Chapters on Tai Chi Ch'uan.* Brooklyn, NY: Sweet Ch'I Press, 1984.

Mitchell, Damo. *Fundamentals of Using the Kua in Nei Jia*, video.

McCluggage, Denise. *The Centered Skier.* Waitsfield, VT: Tempest Books, 1997.

Reeves, Steve, with James A Petersen. *Power Walking.* Indianapolis, IN: Bobbs-Merrill, 1982.

Rosenfeld, Arthur. *Tai Chi, The Perfect Exercise.* Boston: Da Capo Press, 2013.

Sabini, Meredith. *The Earth Has a Soul, The Nature Writings of C.G. Jung.* Berkeley, CA: North Atlantic Books, 2005.

Tseng, Yun Xiang. *Master Within.* Dayton, OH: In the Garden Publishing, 2012.

Tsu, Lao, Gia-Fu Feng, Jane English, Toinette Lippe. *Tao Te Ching.* New York: Vintage Books, 2011.

Tsung Hwa, Jou, Lao Ma. *Taijiquan Classics: Compilation and Comparisons.* Chapel Hill, NC: Black Bamboo Pavilion, Magic Tortoise Taijiquan School, 2002.

Tzu, Lao, and Charles Muller. *Tao Te Ching.* New York: Barnes & Noble, 2005.

Watts, Alan, and Al Chung-Liang Huang. *Tao: The Watercourse Way.* New York: Pantheon Books, 1975.

Wayne, Peter M, and Mark L. Fuerst. *The Harvard Medical School Guide to Tai Chi.* Boston: Shambhala Publications, 2013.

Wile, Douglas. *Lost T'ai-Chi Classics from the Late Ch'ing Dynasty.* Albany: State Univ. of New York Press, 1996.

Wilson, Carol Ann. *Still Point of the Turning World.* Portland, OR: Amber Lotus Publishing, 2009.

Xin, Chen. *The Illustrated Canon of Chen Family Taijiquan.* Maroubra, Australia: INBI Matrix Pty Ltd, 2007.

Yang, Yang. Taijiquan: *The Art of Nurturing, the Science of Power.* Champaign, IL: Zhenwu Publishing, 2005.

Acknowledgment

A special thank you to Maria Valladarez for capturing, through her ink drawings, the spirit and message present in The Gift of Tai Chi.

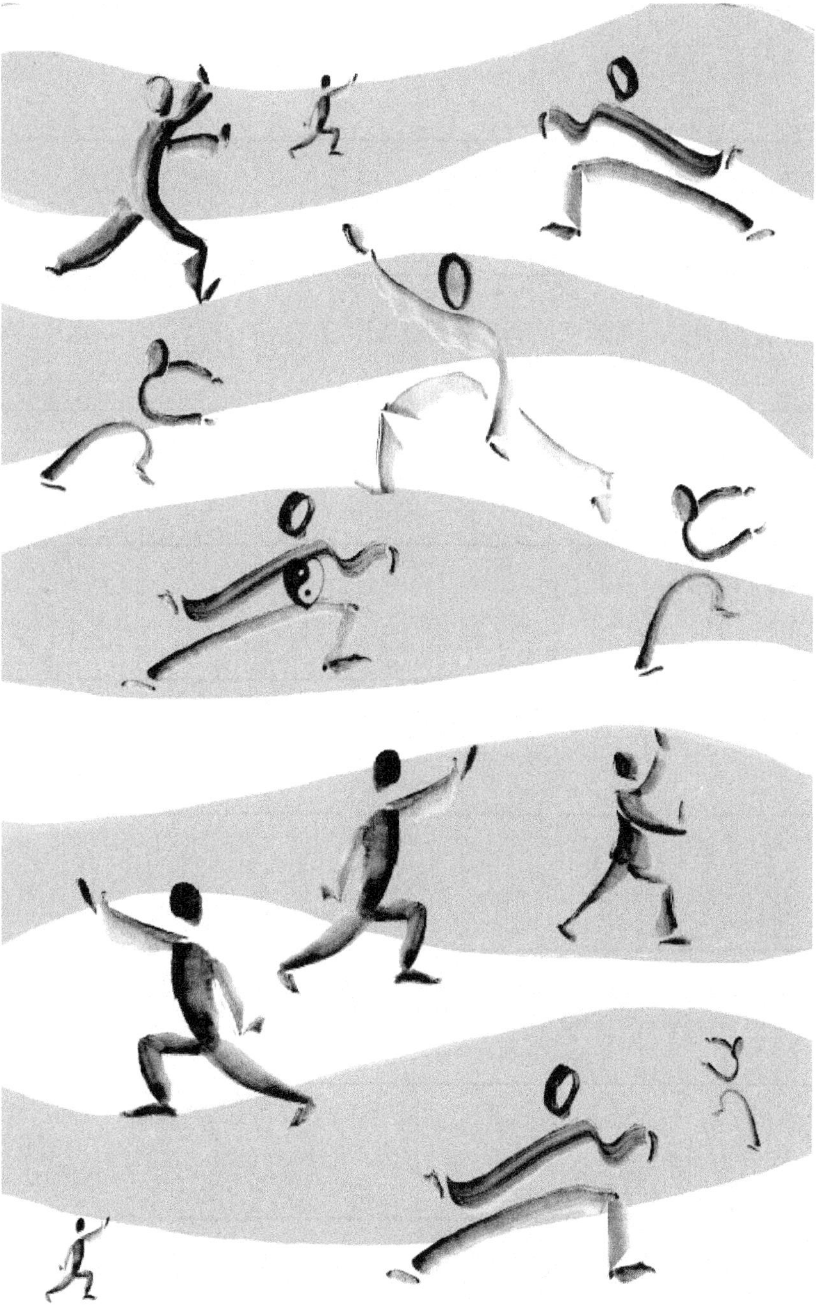

NOTES

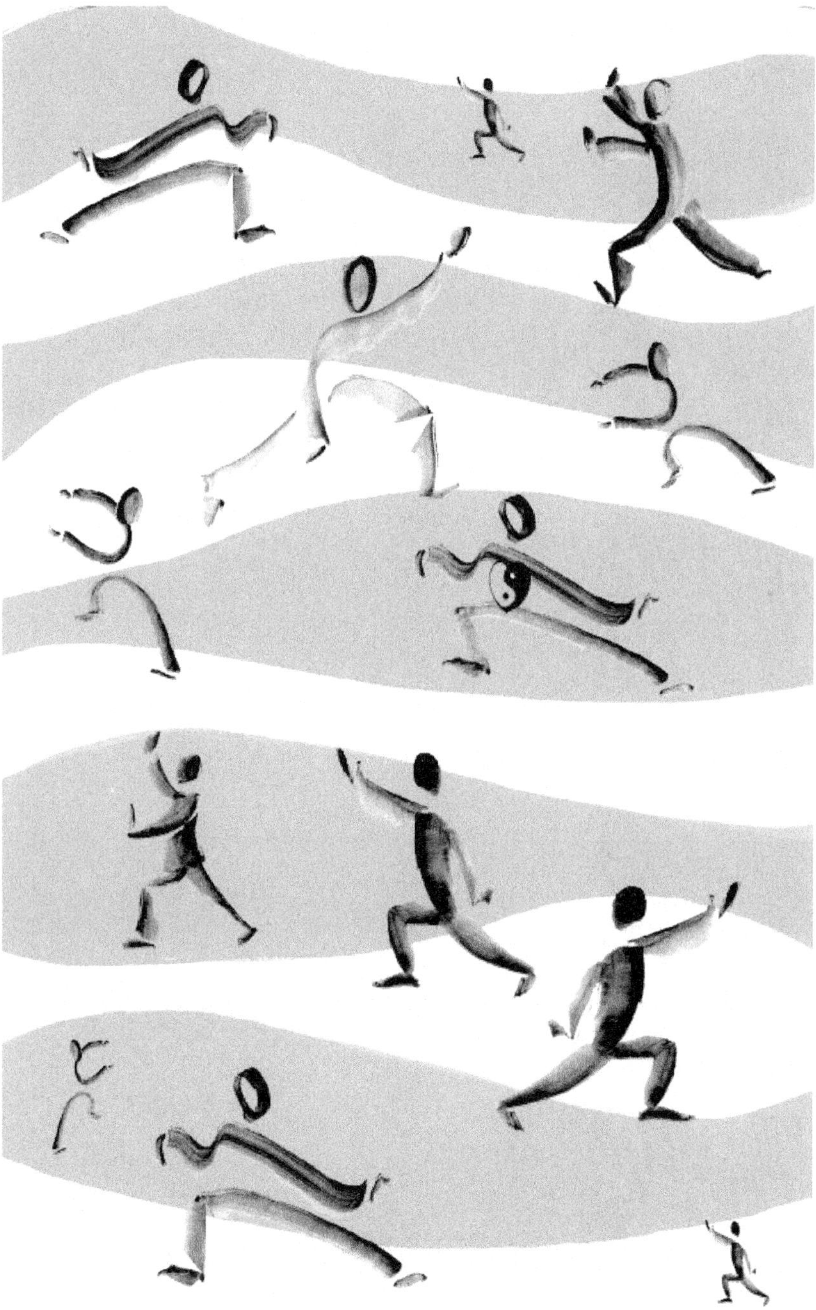